CALIFORNIA
Animal Tracks

Identification Record Book
- Companion Field Guide -

Hello Wild

Your Feedback is Appreciated!!!

Please consider leaving us "5 Stars" on your
Amazon review.

Thank you!

This Animal Track Identification Book
Belongs To:

_____

General

Date: _____   Location: _____

Environment: ◯ Mud   ◯ Snow   ◯ Soft Garden Soil   ◯ Sand

Time of Day: ◯ Morning   ◯ Midday   ◯ Evening   ◯ Time_____

Front Toes: ◯ Five   ◯ Four   ◯ Three   ◯ Two

Rear Toes: ◯ Five   ◯ Four   ◯ Three   ◯ Two

Track Symmetry: ◯ Symmetric   ◯ Asymmetric

Claws / Nails: ◯ Visible   ◯ Not Visible   Webbing: ◯ Yes   ◯ No

Surroundings:_____

Movement Pattern: ◯ Zig-Zaggler   ◯ Trot   ◯ Lope   ◯ Gallop

Notes:_____

Canine

Wolf

FRONT   REAR

Biggest in this group with a long (4") and wide print.

Coyote
FRONT   REAR

Slightly smaller than wolves with print more narrow (2.5 to 3.5").

Fox
FRONT   REAR

Smallest in the group with print (2 to 3") and fuzzy around edges.

Dog
FRONT   REAR

Similar to wolf/coyote with thicker nails.

Feline

Cougar / Mountain Lion

FRONT   REAR

Largest in the group (greater than 3"). Size of domestic dog.

Lynx

FRONT   REAR

Same as cougar but smaller in size and not as defined due to fur around paws.

Bobcat
FRONT   REAR

Smaller tracks (2"). Often confused with coyote or fox but lacks nails. Round shape.

House Cat

FRONT   REAR

Small (1 to 1.5"). Similar to domestic dog, meander when walking.

Bird

Crow
FRONT   REAR

Standard bird track: 3 forward, 1 rear. Print 2-2.5".

Grouse

Small ground birds with only 3 forward toes. Print 2" long.

Turkey

Similar to grouse but much larger prints (4") long.

Duck

Webbing gives its print distinctive shape.

Bear

Black Bear

FRONT   REAR

Has short claws and its toes spread out in a curve over its foot pad. Generally going to be smaller than grizzly bear paw.

Grizzly Bear

FRONT   REAR

Has long claws that extend out further from their toes. Its toes also are held closer together, forming almost a straight line above the foot pad.

Rodent

Beaver

FRONT   REAR
Webbed hind feet with 5 toes (4.5-7"). Sometime 4-toed prints.

Porcupine

FRONT   REAR
Usually only see pads in prints (1-2"). Pigeon-toed.

Muskrat

FRONT   REAR
Hand-like like raccoon but smaller (2.3").

Mouse

FRONT   REAR
Larger back feet (1.5 - 2"), smaller front feet (0.25-0.5").

Squirrel
FRONT   REAR
Larger back feet (1.5-2"), smaller front feet (1-1.5").

Hoof

Mountain Goat

FRONT   REAR
Have toes that spread when they step, creating a distinctive V shape at the top of their print.

Bighorn Sheep

FRONT   REAR
Similar to deer but with straighter edges and less pointed. More blocky and less shaped like a heart.

Wild Hog

FRONT   REAR
Often confused with deer but toes are wider, rounder and blunter and don't come to a point. Have dew claw that rests slightly outside print.

Reptile / Amphibian

Alligator

FRONT
REAR
Large feet with four toes on front prints and five toes on rear prints. Front are wide in heel, rear are longer, narrow and pointed heel.

Lizard

FRONT   REAR
Lightweight and don't leave much of a track. Might leave small scuff from feet and small tail drag.

Frog

FRONT   REAR
Have four bulbous toes in front and five in hind prints. Front toes point slightly inward producing a "K" shaped print, while rear toes slope upward and outward.

Other Common

Raccoon

FRONT
REAR
Five toes resembles hand of a baby. Front print smaller (1-3") with C-shaped heel pad. Rear print longer (1.5-4") heel pad.

Opossum

FRONT   REAR
Five fingers and human hand shape. Opposable thumbs on hind feet.

Rabbit
REAR

FRONT
Larger hind feet, smaller front feet. Hoppers producing a "Y" shaped track.

Skunk

FRONT   REAR
Five toes on their hind and front feet. Front and rear are approximately same size. Claws show up in many prints.

Otter

FRONT   REAR
Five toes and short claws give their prints a pointed look. Toes are partially webbed.

Armadillo
REAR

FRONT
Four long toe prints with sharp claw at tip. Front print show distinct "V" between middle toes.

Sketch

Sketch / Notes

General

Date: _____ Location: _____

Environment: ⭘ Mud ⭘ Snow ⭘ Soft Garden Soil ⭘ Sand

Time of Day: ⭘ Morning ⭘ Midday ⭘ Evening ⭘ Time_____

Front Toes: ⭘ Five ⭘ Four ⭘ Three ⭘ Two

Rear Toes: ⭘ Five ⭘ Four ⭘ Three ⭘ Two

Track Symmetry: ⭘ Symmetric ⭘ Asymmetric

Claws / Nails: ⭘ Visible ⭘ Not Visible Webbing: ⭘ Yes ⭘ No

Surroundings: _____

Movement Pattern: ⭘ Zig-Zaggler ⭘ Trot ⭘ Lope ⭘ Gallop

Notes: _____

Canine

Wolf

FRONT REAR

Biggest in this group with a long (4") and wide print.

Coyote

FRONT REAR

Slightly smaller than wolves with print more narrow (2.5 to 3.5").

Fox

FRONT REAR

Smallest in the group with print (2 to 3") and fuzzy around edges.

Dog

FRONT REAR

Similar to wolf/coyote with thicker nails.

Feline

Cougar / Mountain Lion

FRONT REAR

Largest in the group (greater than 3"). Size of domestic dog.

Lynx

FRONT REAR

Same as cougar but smaller in size and not as defined due to fur around paws.

Bobcat

FRONT REAR

Smaller tracks (2"). Often confused with coyote or fox but lacks nails. Round shape.

House Cat

FRONT REAR

Small (1 to 1.5"). Similar to domestic dog, meander when walking.

Bird

Crow

Standard bird track: 3 forward, 1 rear. Print 2-2.5".

Grouse

Small ground birds with only 3 forward toes. Print 2" long.

Turkey

Similar to grouse but much larger prints (4") long.

Duck

Webbing gives its print distinctive shape.

Bear

Black Bear

FRONT REAR

Has short claws and its toes spread out in a curve over its foot pad. Generally going to be smaller than grizzly bear paw.

Grizzly Bear

FRONT REAR

Has long claws that extend out further from their toes. Its toes also are held closer together, forming almost a straight line above the foot pad.

Rodent

Beaver

FRONT   REAR

Webbed hind feet with 5 toes (4.5-7"). Sometime 4-toed prints.

Porcupine

FRONT   REAR

Usually only see pads in prints (1-2"). Pigeon-toed.

Muskrat
FRONT   REAR

Hand-like like raccoon but smaller (2.3").

Mouse

FRONT   REAR

Larger back feet (1.5 - 2"), smaller front feet (0.25-0.5").

Squirrel

FRONT   REAR

Larger back feet (1.5-2"), smaller front feet (1-1.5").

Hoof

Mountain Goat

FRONT   REAR

Have toes that spread when they step, creating a distinctive V shape at the top of their print.

Bighorn Sheep

FRONT   REAR

Similar to deer but with straighter edges and less pointed. More blocky and less shaped like a heart.

Wild Hog

FRONT   REAR

Often confused with deer but toes are wider, rounder and blunter and don't come to a point. Have dew claw that rests slightly outside print.

Reptile / Amphibian

Alligator

FRONT

REAR

Large feet with four toes on front prints and five toes on rear prints. Front are wide in heel, rear are longer, narrow and pointed heel.

Lizard

FRONT   REAR

Lightweight and don't leave much of a track. Might leave small scuff from feet and small tail drag.

Frog

FRONT   REAR

Have four bulbous toes in front and five in hind prints. Front toes point slightly inward producing a "K" shaped print, while rear toes slope upward and outward.

Other Common

Raccoon

FRONT

REAR

Five toes resembles hand of a baby. Front print smaller (1-3") with C-shaped heel pad. Rear print longer (1.5-4") heel pad.

Opossum

FRONT   REAR

Five fingers and human hand shape. Opposable thumbs on hind feet.

Rabbit
REAR

FRONT

Larger hind feet, smaller front feet. Hoppers producing a "Y" shaped track.

Skunk

FRONT   REAR

Five toes on their hind and front feet. Front and rear are approximately same size. Claws show up in many prints.

Otter

FRONT   REAR

Five toes and short claws give their prints a pointed look. Toes are partially webbed.

Armadillo
REAR

FRONT

Four long toe prints with sharp claw at tip. Front print show distinct "V" between middle toes.

Sketch / Notes

Sketch

_____
_____
_____
_____
_____
_____
_____
_____
_____
_____
_____

General

Date: _____ Location: _____

Environment: ○ Mud ○ Snow ○ Soft Garden Soil ○ Sand

Time of Day: ○ Morning ○ Midday ○ Evening ○ Time_____

Front Toes: ○ Five ○ Four ○ Three ○ Two

Rear Toes: ○ Five ○ Four ○ Three ○ Two

Track Symmetry: ○ Symmetric ○ Asymmetric

Claws / Nails: ○ Visible ○ Not Visible   Webbing: ○ Yes ○ No

Surroundings: _____

Movement Pattern: ○ Zig-Zaggler ○ Trot ○ Lope ○ Gallop

Notes: _____

Canine

Wolf

FRONT   REAR

Biggest in this group with a long (4") and wide print.

Coyote
FRONT   REAR

Slightly smaller than wolves with print more narrow (2.5 to 3.5").

Fox

FRONT   REAR

Smallest in the group with print (2 to 3") and fuzzy around edges.

Dog

FRONT   REAR

Similar to wolf/coyote with thicker nails.

Feline

Cougar / Mountain Lion
FRONT   REAR

Largest in the group (greater than 3"). Size of domestic dog.

Lynx

FRONT   REAR

Same as cougar but smaller in size and not as defined due to fur around paws.

Bobcat

FRONT   REAR

Smaller tracks (2"). Often confused with coyote or fox but lacks nails. Round shape.

House Cat

FRONT   REAR

Small (1 to 1.5"). Similar to domestic dog, meander when walking.

Bird

Crow

Standard bird track: 3 forward, 1 rear. Print 2-2.5".

Grouse

Small ground birds with only 3 forward toes. Print 2" long.

Turkey
Similar to grouse but much larger prints (4") long.

Duck
Webbing gives its print distinctive shape.

Bear

Black Bear

FRONT   REAR

Has short claws and its toes spread out in a curve over its foot pad. Generally going to be smaller than grizzly bear paw.

Grizzly Bear

FRONT   REAR

Has long claws that extend out further from their toes. Its toes also are held closer together, forming almost a straight line above the foot pad.

Rodent

Beaver

FRONT | REAR
Webbed hind feet with 5 toes (4.5-7"). Sometime 4-toed prints.

Porcupine

FRONT | REAR
Usually only see pads in prints (1-2"). Pigeon-toed.

Muskrat

FRONT | REAR
Hand-like like raccoon but smaller (2.3").

Mouse

FRONT | REAR
Larger back feet (1.5 - 2"), smaller front feet (0.25-0.5").

Squirrel

FRONT | REAR
Larger back feet (1.5-2"), smaller front feet (1-1.5").

Hoof

Mountain Goat

FRONT | REAR
Have toes that spread when they step, creating a distinctive V shape at the top of their print.

Bighorn Sheep
FRONT | REAR
Similar to deer but with straighter edges and less pointed. More blocky and less shaped like a heart.

Wild Hog

FRONT | REAR
Often confused with deer but toes are wider, rounder and blunter and don't come to a point. Have dew claw that rests slightly outside print.

Reptile / Amphibian

Alligator

FRONT
REAR
Large feet with four toes on front prints and five toes on rear prints. Front are wide in heel, rear are longer, narrow and pointed heel.

Lizard

FRONT | REAR
Lightweight and don't leave much of a track. Might leave small scuff from feet and small tail drag.

Frog

FRONT | REAR
Have four bulbous toes in front and five in hind prints. Front toes point slightly inward producing a "K" shaped print, while rear toes slope upward and outward.

Other Common

Raccoon

FRONT
REAR
Five toes resembles hand of a baby. Front print smaller (1-3") with C-shaped heel pad. Rear print longer (1.5-4") heel pad.

Opossum

FRONT | REAR
Five fingers and human hand shape. Opposable thumbs on hind feet.

Rabbit
REAR
FRONT
Larger hind feet, smaller front feet. Hoppers producing a "Y" shaped track.

Skunk

FRONT | REAR
Five toes on their hind and front feet. Front and rear are approximately same size. Claws show up in many prints.

Otter

FRONT | REAR
Five toes and short claws give their prints a pointed look. Toes are partially webbed.

Armadillo

REAR
FRONT
Four long toe prints with sharp claw at tip. Front print show distinct "V" between middle toes.

Sketch / Notes

Sketch

General

Date: _____   Location: _____

Environment: ◯ Mud   ◯ Snow   ◯ Soft Garden Soil   ◯ Sand

Time of Day: ◯ Morning   ◯ Midday   ◯ Evening   ◯ Time_____

Front Toes: ◯ Five   ◯ Four   ◯ Three   ◯ Two

Rear Toes: ◯ Five   ◯ Four   ◯ Three   ◯ Two

Track Symmetry: ◯ Symmetric   ◯ Asymmetric

Claws / Nails: ◯ Visible   ◯ Not Visible   Webbing: ◯ Yes   ◯ No

Surroundings: _____

Movement Pattern: ◯ Zig-Zaggler   ◯ Trot   ◯ Lope   ◯ Gallop

Notes: _____

Canine

Wolf

FRONT   REAR

Biggest in this group with a long (4") and wide print.

Coyote
FRONT   REAR

Slightly smaller than wolves with print more narrow (2.5 to 3.5").

Fox
FRONT   REAR

Smallest in the group with print (2 to 3") and fuzzy around edges.

Dog
FRONT   REAR

Similar to wolf/coyote with thicker nails.

Feline

Cougar / Mountain Lion
FRONT   REAR

Largest in the group (greater than 3"). Size of domestic dog.

Lynx

FRONT   REAR

Same as cougar but smaller in size and not as defined due to fur around paws.

Bobcat
FRONT   REAR

Smaller tracks (2"). Often confused with coyote or fox but lacks nails. Round shape.

House Cat

FRONT   REAR

Small (1 to 1.5"). Similar to domestic dog, meander when walking.

Bird

Crow
FRONT   REAR

Standard bird track: 3 forward, 1 rear. Print 2-2.5".

Grouse
FRONT   REAR

Small ground birds with only 3 forward toes. Print 2" long.

Turkey

Similar to grouse but much larger prints (4") long.

Duck

Webbing gives its print distinctive shape.

Bear

Black Bear

FRONT   REAR

Has short claws and its toes spread out in a curve over its foot pad. Generally going to be smaller than grizzly bear paw.

Grizzly Bear

FRONT   REAR

Has long claws that extend out further from their toes. Its toes also are held closer together, forming almost a straight line above the foot pad.

Rodent

Beaver

FRONT   REAR

Webbed hind feet with 5 toes (4.5-7"). Sometime 4-toed prints.

Porcupine

FRONT REAR

Usually only see pads in prints (1-2"). Pigeon-toed.

Muskrat

FRONT   REAR

Hand-like like raccoon but smaller (2.3").

Mouse
FRONT   REAR

Larger back feet (1.5 - 2"), smaller front feet (0.25-0.5").

Squirrel

FRONT   REAR

Larger back feet (1.5-2"), smaller front feet (1-1.5").

Hoof

Mountain Goat

FRONT   REAR

Have toes that spread when they step, creating a distinctive V shape at the top of their print.

Bighorn Sheep

FRONT   REAR

Similar to deer but with straighter edges and less pointed. More blocky and less shaped like a heart.

Wild Hog

FRONT   REAR

Often confused with deer but toes are wider, rounder and blunter and don't come to a point. Have dew claw that rests slightly outside print.

Reptile / Amphibian

Alligator

FRONT

REAR

Large feet with four toes on front prints and five toes on rear prints. Front are wide in heel, rear are longer, narrow and pointed heel.

Lizard

FRONT   REAR

Lightweight and don't leave much of a track. Might leave small scuff from feet and small tail drag.

Frog

FRONT   REAR

Have four bulbous toes in front and five in hind prints. Front toes point slightly inward producing a "K" shaped print, while rear toes slope upward and outward.

Other Common

Raccoon

FRONT

REAR

Five toes resembles hand of a baby. Front print smaller (1-3") with C-shaped heel pad. Rear print longer (1.5-4') heel pad.

Opossum

FRONT   REAR

Five fingers and human hand shape. Opposable thumbs on hind feet .

Rabbit
REAR

FRONT

Larger hind feet, smaller front feet. Hoppers producing a "Y" shaped track.

Skunk

FRONT

REAR

Five toes on their hind and front feet. Front and rear are approximately same size. Claws show up in many prints.

Otter

FRONT   REAR

Five toes and short claws give their prints a pointed look. Toes are partially webbed.

Armadillo
REAR

FRONT

Four long toe prints with sharp claw at tip. Front print show distinct "V" between middle toes.

Sketch

Sketch / Notes

General

Date:_____ Location:_____

Environment: ○ Mud ○ Snow ○ Soft Garden Soil ○ Sand

Time of Day: ○ Morning ○ Midday ○ Evening ○ Time_____

Front Toes: ○ Five ○ Four ○ Three ○ Two

Rear Toes: ○ Five ○ Four ○ Three ○ Two

Track Symmetry: ○ Symmetric ○ Asymmetric

Claws / Nails: ○ Visible ○ Not Visible   Webbing: ○ Yes ○ No

Surroundings:_____

Movement Pattern: ○ Zig-Zaggler ○ Trot ○ Lope ○ Gallop

Notes:_____

Canine

Wolf
FRONT   REAR

Biggest in this group with a long (4") and wide print.

Coyote
FRONT   REAR

Slightly smaller than wolves with print more narrow (2.5 to 3.5").

Fox
FRONT   REAR

Smallest in the group with print (2 to 3") and fuzzy around edges.

Dog
FRONT   REAR

Similar to wolf/coyote with thicker nails.

Feline

Cougar / Mountain Lion
FRONT   REAR

Largest in the group (greater than 3"). Size of domestic dog.

Lynx
FRONT   REAR

Same as cougar but smaller in size and not as defined due to fur around paws.

Bobcat
FRONT   REAR

Smaller tracks (2"). Often confused with coyote or fox but lacks nails. Round shape.

House Cat
FRONT   REAR

Small (1 to 1.5"). Similar to domestic dog, meander when walking.

Bird

Crow
Standard bird track: 3 forward, 1 rear. Print 2-2.5".

Grouse
Small ground birds with only 3 forward toes. Print 2" long.

Turkey
Similar to grouse but much larger prints (4") long.

Duck
Webbing gives its print distinctive shape.

Bear

Black Bear
FRONT   REAR

Has short claws and its toes spread out in a curve over its foot pad. Generally going to be smaller than grizzly bear paw.

Grizzly Bear
FRONT   REAR

Has long claws that extend out further from their toes. Its toes also are held closer together, forming almost a straight line above the foot pad.

Rodent

Beaver

FRONT   REAR
Webbed hind feet with 5 toes (4.5-7"). Sometime 4-toed prints.

Porcupine

FRONT   REAR
Usually only see pads in prints (1-2"). Pigeon-toed.

Muskrat

FRONT   REAR
Hand-like like raccoon but smaller (2.3").

Mouse

FRONT   REAR
Larger back feet (1.5 - 2"), smaller front feet (0.25-0.5").

Squirrel

FRONT   REAR
Larger back feet (1.5-2"), smaller front feet (1-1.5").

Hoof

Mountain Goat

FRONT   REAR
Have toes that spread when they step, creating a distinctive V shape at the top of their print.

Bighorn Sheep

FRONT   REAR
Similar to deer but with straighter edges and less pointed. More blocky and less shaped like a heart.

Wild Hog

FRONT   REAR
Often confused with deer but toes are wider, rounder and blunter and don't come to a point. Have dew claw that rests slightly outside print.

Reptile / Amphibian

Alligator

FRONT
REAR
Large feet with four toes on front prints and five toes on rear prints. Front are wide in heel, rear are longer, narrow and pointed heel.

Lizard

FRONT   REAR
Lightweight and don't leave much of a track. Might leave small scuff from feet and small tail drag.

Frog

FRONT   REAR
Have four bulbous toes in front and five in hind prints. Front toes point slightly inward producing a "K" shaped print, while rear toes slope upward and outward.

Other Common

Raccoon

FRONT
REAR
Five toes resembles hand of a baby. Front print smaller (1-3") with C-shaped heel pad. Rear print longer (1.5-4') heel pad.

Opossum

FRONT   REAR
Five fingers and human hand shape. Opposable thumbs on hind feet.

Rabbit
REAR

FRONT
Larger hind feet, smaller front feet. Hoppers producing a "Y" shaped track.

Skunk

FRONT
REAR
Five toes on their hind and front feet. Front and rear are approximately same size. Claws show up in many prints.

Otter

FRONT   REAR
Five toes and short claws give their prints a pointed look. Toes are partially webbed.

Armadillo
REAR

FRONT
Four long toe prints with sharp claw at tip. Front print show distinct "V" between middle toes.

Sketch / Notes

Sketch

_____
_____
_____
_____
_____
_____
_____
_____
_____
_____
_____

General

Date: _____   Location: _____

Environment: ◯ Mud   ◯ Snow   ◯ Soft Garden Soil   ◯ Sand

Time of Day: ◯ Morning   ◯ Midday   ◯ Evening   ◯ Time _____

Front Toes: ◯ Five   ◯ Four   ◯ Three   ◯ Two

Rear Toes: ◯ Five   ◯ Four   ◯ Three   ◯ Two

Track Symmetry: ◯ Symmetric   ◯ Asymmetric

Claws / Nails: ◯ Visible   ◯ Not Visible   Webbing: ◯ Yes   ◯ No

Surroundings: _____

Movement Pattern: ◯ Zig-Zaggler   ◯ Trot   ◯ Lope   ◯ Gallop

Notes: _____

Canine

Wolf
FRONT   REAR

Biggest in this group with a long (4") and wide print.

Coyote
FRONT   REAR

Slightly smaller than wolves with print more narrow (2.5 to 3.5").

Fox
FRONT   REAR

Smallest in the group with print (2 to 3") and fuzzy around edges.

Dog
FRONT   REAR

Similar to wolf/coyote with thicker nails.

Feline

Cougar / Mountain Lion
FRONT   REAR

Largest in the group (greater than 3"). Size of domestic dog.

Lynx
FRONT   REAR

Same as cougar but smaller in size and not as defined due to fur around paws.

Bobcat
FRONT   REAR

Smaller tracks (2"). Often confused with coyote or fox but lacks nails. Round shape.

House Cat
FRONT   REAR

Small (1 to 1.5"). Similar to domestic dog, meander when walking.

Bird

Crow
Standard bird track: 3 forward, 1 rear. Print 2-2.5".

Grouse
Small ground birds with only 3 forward toes. Print 2" long.

Turkey
Similar to grouse but much larger prints (4") long.

Duck

Webbing gives its print distinctive shape.

Bear

Black Bear

FRONT   REAR

Has short claws and its toes spread out in a curve over its foot pad. Generally going to be smaller than grizzly bear paw.

Grizzly Bear

FRONT   REAR

Has long claws that extend out further from their toes. Its toes also are held closer together, forming almost a straight line above the foot pad.

Rodent

Beaver

FRONT   REAR
Webbed hind feet with 5 toes (4.5-7"). Sometime 4-toed prints.

Porcupine

FRONT REAR
Usually only see pads in prints (1-2"). Pigeon-toed.

Muskrat

FRONT REAR
Hand-like like raccoon but smaller (2.3").

Mouse
FRONT REAR
Larger back feet (1.5 - 2"), smaller front feet (0.25-0.5").

Squirrel

FRONT   REAR
Larger back feet (1.5-2"), smaller front feet (1-1.5").

Hoof

Mountain Goat

FRONT   REAR
Have toes that spread when they step, creating a distinctive V shape at the top of their print.

Bighorn Sheep

FRONT   REAR
Similar to deer but with straighter edges and less pointed. More blocky and less shaped like a heart.

Wild Hog

FRONT   REAR
Often confused with deer but toes are wider, rounder and blunter and don't come to a point. Have dew claw that rests slightly outside print.

Reptile / Amphibian

Alligator

FRONT
REAR
Large feet with four toes on front prints and five toes on rear prints. Front are wide in heel, rear are longer, narrow and pointed heel.

Lizard

FRONT   REAR
Lightweight and don't leave much of a track. Might leave small scuff from feet and small tail drag.

Frog

FRONT   REAR
Have four bulbous toes in front and five in hind prints. Front toes point slightly inward producing a "K" shaped print, while rear toes slope upward and outward.

Other Common

Raccoon

FRONT
REAR
Five toes resembles hand of a baby. Front print smaller (1-3") with C-shaped heel pad. Rear print longer (1.5-4") heel pad.

Opossum

FRONT   REAR
Five fingers and human hand shape. Opposable thumbs on hind feet.

Rabbit
REAR

FRONT
Larger hind feet, smaller front feet. Hoppers producing a "Y" shaped track.

Skunk

FRONT
REAR
Five toes on their hind and front feet. Front and rear are approximately same size. Claws show up in many prints.

Otter

FRONT   REAR
Five toes and short claws give their prints a pointed look. Toes are partially webbed.

Armadillo
REAR

FRONT
Four long toe prints with sharp claw at tip. Front print show distinct "V" between middle toes.

Sketch

Sketch / Notes

_____
_____
_____
_____
_____
_____
_____
_____
_____
_____
_____

General

Date: _____ Location: _____

Environment: ◯ Mud ◯ Snow ◯ Soft Garden Soil ◯ Sand

Time of Day: ◯ Morning ◯ Midday ◯ Evening ◯ Time _____

Front Toes: ◯ Five ◯ Four ◯ Three ◯ Two

Rear Toes: ◯ Five ◯ Four ◯ Three ◯ Two

Track Symmetry: ◯ Symmetric ◯ Asymmetric

Claws / Nails: ◯ Visible ◯ Not Visible   Webbing: ◯ Yes ◯ No

Surroundings: _____

Movement Pattern: ◯ Zig-Zaggler   ◯ Trot   ◯ Lope   ◯ Gallop

Notes: _____

Canine

Wolf	Coyote	Fox	Dog
FRONT REAR	FRONT REAR	FRONT REAR	FRONT REAR
Biggest in this group with a long (4") and wide print.	Slightly smaller than wolves with print more narrow (2.5 to 3.5").	Smallest in the group with print (2 to 3") and fuzzy around edges.	Similar to wolf/coyote with thicker nails.

Feline

Cougar / Mountain Lion	Lynx	Bobcat	House Cat
FRONT REAR	FRONT REAR	FRONT REAR	FRONT REAR
Largest in the group (greater than 3"). Size of domestic dog.	Same as cougar but smaller in size and not as defined due to fur around paws.	Smaller tracks (2"). Often confused with coyote or fox but lacks nails. Round shape.	Small (1 to 1.5"). Similar to domestic dog, meander when walking.

Bird

Crow	Grouse	Turkey	Duck
Standard bird track: 3 forward, 1 rear. Print 2-2.5".	Small ground birds with only 3 forward toes. Print 2" long.	Similar to grouse but much larger prints (4") long.	Webbing gives its print distinctive shape.

Bear

Black Bear

FRONT   REAR

Has short claws and its toes spread out in a curve over its foot pad. Generally going to be smaller than grizzly bear paw.

Grizzly Bear

FRONT   REAR

Has long claws that extend out further from their toes. Its toes also are held closer together, forming almost a straight line above the foot pad.

Rodent

Beaver

FRONT   REAR

Webbed hind feet with 5 toes (4.5-7"). Sometime 4-toed prints.

Porcupine

FRONT   REAR

Usually only see pads in prints (1-2"). Pigeon-toed.

Muskrat

FRONT   REAR

Hand-like like raccoon but smaller (2.3").

Mouse

FRONT   REAR

Larger back feet (1.5 - 2"), smaller front feet (0.25-0.5").

Squirrel

FRONT   REAR

Larger back feet (1.5-2"), smaller front feet (1-1.5")

Hoof

Mountain Goat

FRONT   REAR

Have toes that spread when they step, creating a distinctive V shape at the top of their print.

Bighorn Sheep

FRONT   REAR

Similar to deer but with straighter edges and less pointed. More blocky and less shaped like a heart.

Wild Hog

FRONT   REAR

Often confused with deer but toes are wider, rounder and blunter and don't come to a point. Have dew claw that rests slightly outside print.

Reptile / Amphibian

Alligator

FRONT   REAR

Large feet with four toes on front prints and five toes on rear prints. Front are wide in heel, rear are longer, narrow and pointed heel.

Lizard

FRONT   REAR

Lightweight and don't leave much of a track. Might leave small scuff from feet and small tail drag.

Frog

FRONT   REAR

Have four bulbous toes in front and five in hind prints. Front toes point slightly inward producing a "K" shaped print, while rear toes slope upward and outward.

Other Common

Raccoon

FRONT   REAR

Five toes resembles hand of a baby. Front print smaller (1-3") with C-shaped heel pad. Rear print longer (1.5-4") heel pad.

Opossum

FRONT   REAR

Five fingers and human hand shape. Opposable thumbs on hind feet .

Rabbit
REAR

FRONT

Larger hind feet, smaller front feet. Hoppers producing a "Y" shaped track.

Skunk
FRONT   REAR

Five toes on their hind and front feet. Front and rear are approximately same size. Claws show up in many prints.

Otter

FRONT   REAR

Five toes and short claws give their prints a pointed look. Toes are partially webbed.

Armadillo
REAR
FRONT

Four long toe prints with sharp claw at tip. Front print show distinct "V" between middle toes.

Sketch

Sketch / Notes

General

Date: _____ Location: _____

Environment: ○ Mud ○ Snow ○ Soft Garden Soil ○ Sand

Time of Day: ○ Morning ○ Midday ○ Evening ○ Time_____

Front Toes: ○ Five ○ Four ○ Three ○ Two

Rear Toes: ○ Five ○ Four ○ Three ○ Two

Track Symmetry: ○ Symmetric ○ Asymmetric

Claws / Nails: ○ Visible ○ Not Visible Webbing: ○ Yes ○ No

Surroundings: _____

Movement Pattern: ○ Zig-Zaggler ○ Trot ○ Lope ○ Gallop

Notes: _____

Canine

Wolf

FRONT   REAR

Biggest in this group with a long (4") and wide print.

Coyote
FRONT   REAR

Slightly smaller than wolves with print more narrow (2.5 to 3.5").

Fox
FRONT   REAR

Smallest in the group with print (2 to 3") and fuzzy around edges.

Dog
FRONT   REAR

Similar to wolf/coyote with thicker nails.

Feline

Cougar / Mountain Lion

FRONT   REAR

Largest in the group (greater than 3"). Size of domestic dog.

Lynx

FRONT   REAR

Same as cougar but smaller in size and not as defined due to fur around paws.

Bobcat

FRONT   REAR

Smaller tracks (2"). Often confused with coyote or fox but lacks nails. Round shape.

House Cat

FRONT   REAR

Small (1 to 1.5"). Similar to domestic dog, meander when walking.

Bird

Crow

Standard bird track: 3 forward, 1 rear. Print 2-2.5".

Grouse

Small ground birds with only 3 forward toes. Print 2" long.

Turkey

Similar to grouse but much larger prints (4") long.

Duck

Webbing gives its print distinctive shape.

Bear

Black Bear

FRONT   REAR

Has short claws and its toes spread out in a curve over its foot pad. Generally going to be smaller than grizzly bear paw.

Grizzly Bear

FRONT   REAR

Has long claws that extend out further from their toes. Its toes also are held closer together, forming almost a straight line above the foot pad.

Rodent

Beaver	Porcupine	Muskrat	Mouse	Squirrel
FRONT REAR	FRONT REAR	FRONT REAR	FRONT REAR	FRONT REAR
Webbed hind feet with 5 toes (4.5-7"). Sometime 4-toed prints.	Usually only see pads in prints (1-2"). Pigeon-toed.	Hand-like like raccoon but smaller (2.3").	Larger back feet (1.5 - 2"), smaller front feet (0.25-0.5").	Larger back feet (1.5-2"), smaller front feet (1-1.5").

Hoof

Mountain Goat FRONT REAR — Have toes that spread when they step, creating a distinctive V shape at the top of their print.

Bighorn Sheep FRONT REAR — Similar to deer but with straighter edges and less pointed. More blocky and less shaped like a heart.

Wild Hog FRONT REAR — Often confused with deer but toes are wider, rounder and blunter and don't come to a point. Have dew claw that rests slightly outside print.

Reptile / Amphibian

Alligator FRONT REAR — Large feet with four toes on front prints and five toes on rear prints. Front are wide in heel, rear are longer, narrow and pointed heel.

Lizard FRONT REAR — Lightweight and don't leave much of a track. Might leave small scuff from feet and small tail drag.

Frog FRONT REAR — Have four bulbous toes in front and five in hind prints. Front toes point slightly inward producing a "K" shaped print, while rear toes slope upward and outward.

Other Common

Raccoon FRONT REAR — Five toes resembles hand of a baby. Front print smaller (1-3") with C-shaped heel pad. Rear print longer (1.5-4") heel pad.

Opossum FRONT REAR — Five fingers and human hand shape. Opposable thumbs on hind feet.

Rabbit REAR FRONT — Larger hind feet, smaller front feet. Hoppers producing a "Y" shaped track.

Skunk FRONT REAR — Five toes on their hind and front feet. Front and rear are approximately same size. Claws show up in many prints.

Otter FRONT REAR — Five toes and short claws give their prints a pointed look. Toes are partially webbed.

Armadillo REAR FRONT — Four long toe prints with sharp claw at tip. Front print show distinct "V" between middle toes.

Sketch

Sketch / Notes

_____
_____
_____
_____
_____
_____
_____
_____
_____
_____
_____

General

Date: _____ Location: _____

Environment: ⭘ Mud ⭘ Snow ⭘ Soft Garden Soil ⭘ Sand

Time of Day: ⭘ Morning ⭘ Midday ⭘ Evening ⭘ Time_____

Front Toes: ⭘ Five ⭘ Four ⭘ Three ⭘ Two

Rear Toes: ⭘ Five ⭘ Four ⭘ Three ⭘ Two

Track Symmetry: ⭘ Symmetric ⭘ Asymmetric

Claws / Nails: ⭘ Visible ⭘ Not Visible   Webbing: ⭘ Yes ⭘ No

Surroundings: _____

Movement Pattern: ⭘ Zig-Zaggler ⭘ Trot ⭘ Lope ⭘ Gallop

Notes: _____

Canine

Wolf

FRONT   REAR

Biggest in this group with a long (4") and wide print.

Coyote
FRONT   REAR

Slightly smaller than wolves with print more narrow (2.5 to 3.5").

Fox
FRONT   REAR

Smallest in the group with print (2 to 3") and fuzzy around edges.

Dog

FRONT   REAR

Similar to wolf/coyote with thicker nails.

Feline

Cougar / Mountain Lion

FRONT   REAR

Largest in the group (greater than 3"). Size of domestic dog.

Lynx

FRONT   REAR

Same as cougar but smaller in size and not as defined due to fur around paws.

Bobcat

FRONT   REAR

Smaller tracks (2"). Often confused with coyote or fox but lacks nails. Round shape.

House Cat

FRONT   REAR

Small (1 to 1.5"). Similar to domestic dog, meander when walking.

Bird

Crow

Standard bird track: 3 forward, 1 rear. Print 2-2.5".

Grouse

Small ground birds with only 3 forward toes. Print 2" long.

Turkey

Similar to grouse but much larger prints (4") long.

Duck

Webbing gives its print distinctive shape.

Bear

Black Bear
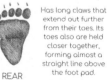
FRONT   REAR

Has short claws and its toes spread out in a curve over its foot pad. Generally going to be smaller than grizzly bear paw.

Grizzly Bear
FRONT   REAR

Has long claws that extend out further from their toes. Its toes also are held closer together, forming almost a straight line above the foot pad.

Rodent

Beaver

FRONT REAR
Webbed hind feet with 5 toes (4.5-7"). Sometime 4-toed prints.

Porcupine

FRONT REAR
Usually only see pads in prints (1-2"). Pigeon-toed.

Muskrat

FRONT REAR
Hand-like like raccoon but smaller (2.3").

Mouse

FRONT REAR
Larger back feet (1.5 - 2"), smaller front feet (0.25-0.5").

Squirrel

FRONT REAR
Larger back feet (1.5-2"), smaller front feet (1-1.5").

Hoof

Mountain Goat

FRONT REAR
Have toes that spread when they step, creating a distinctive V shape at the top of their print.

Bighorn Sheep

FRONT REAR
Similar to deer but with straighter edges and less pointed. More blocky and less shaped like a heart.

Wild Hog

FRONT REAR
Often confused with deer but toes are wider, rounder and blunter and don't come to a point. Have dew claw that rests slightly outside print.

Reptile / Amphibian

Alligator

FRONT
REAR
Large feet with four toes on front prints and five toes on rear prints. Front are wide in heel, rear are longer, narrow and pointed heel.

Lizard

FRONT REAR
Lightweight and don't leave much of a track. Might leave small scuff from feet and small tail drag.

Frog
FRONT REAR
Have four bulbous toes in front and five in hind prints. Front toes point slightly inward producing a "K" shaped print, while rear toes slope upward and outward.

Other Common

Raccoon

FRONT
REAR
Five toes resembles hand of a baby. Front print smaller (1-3") with C-shaped heel pad. Rear print longer (1.5-4") heel pad.

Opossum

FRONT REAR
Five fingers and human hand shape. Opposable thumbs on hind feet.

Rabbit
REAR

FRONT
Larger hind feet, smaller front feet. Hoppers producing a "Y" shaped track.

Skunk

FRONT
REAR
Five toes on their hind and front feet. Front and rear are approximately same size. Claws show up in many prints.

Otter

FRONT REAR
Five toes and short claws give their prints a pointed look. Toes are partially webbed.

Armadillo
REAR

FRONT
Four long toe prints with sharp claw at tip. Front print show distinct 'V' between middle toes.

Sketch

Sketch / Notes

General

Date: _____ Location: _____

Environment: ◯ Mud ◯ Snow ◯ Soft Garden Soil ◯ Sand

Time of Day: ◯ Morning ◯ Midday ◯ Evening ◯ Time _____

Front Toes: ◯ Five ◯ Four ◯ Three ◯ Two

Rear Toes: ◯ Five ◯ Four ◯ Three ◯ Two

Track Symmetry: ◯ Symmetric ◯ Asymmetric

Claws / Nails: ◯ Visible ◯ Not Visible   Webbing: ◯ Yes ◯ No

Surroundings: _____

Movement Pattern: ◯ Zig-Zaggler   ◯ Trot   ◯ Lope   ◯ Gallop

Notes: _____

Canine

Wolf

FRONT   REAR

Biggest in this group with a long (4") and wide print.

Coyote
FRONT   REAR

Slightly smaller than wolves with print more narrow (2.5 to 3.5").

Fox
FRONT   REAR

Smallest in the group with print (2 to 3") and fuzzy around edges.

Dog
FRONT   REAR

Similar to wolf/coyote with thicker nails.

Feline

Cougar / Mountain Lion

FRONT   REAR

Largest in the group (greater than 3"). Size of domestic dog.

Lynx
FRONT   REAR

Same as cougar but smaller in size and not as defined due to fur around paws.

Bobcat

FRONT   REAR

Smaller tracks (2"). Often confused with coyote or fox but lacks nails. Round shape.

House Cat

FRONT   REAR

Small (1 to 1.5"). Similar to domestic dog, meander when walking.

Bird

Crow

Standard bird track: 3 forward, 1 rear. Print 2-2.5".

Grouse

Small ground birds with only 3 forward toes. Print 2" long.

Turkey

Similar to grouse but much larger prints (4") long.

Duck

Webbing gives its print distinctive shape.

Bear

Black Bear

FRONT   REAR

Has short claws and its toes spread out in a curve over its foot pad. Generally going to be smaller than grizzly bear paw.

Grizzly Bear

FRONT   REAR

Has long claws that extend out further from their toes. Its toes also are held closer together, forming almost a straight line above the foot pad.

Rodent

Beaver

FRONT   REAR
Webbed hind feet with 5 toes (4.5-7"). Sometime 4-toed prints.

Porcupine

FRONT   REAR
Usually only see pads in prints (1-2"). Pigeon-toed.

Muskrat
FRONT   REAR
Hand-like like raccoon but smaller (2.3").

Mouse

FRONT   REAR
Larger back feet (1.5 - 2"), smaller front feet (0.25-0.5").

Squirrel

FRONT   REAR
Larger back feet (1.5-2"), smaller front feet (1-1.5").

Hoof

Mountain Goat

FRONT   REAR
Have toes that spread when they step, creating a distinctive V shape at the top of their print.

Bighorn Sheep

FRONT   REAR
Similar to deer but with straighter edges and less pointed. More blocky and less shaped like a heart.

Wild Hog

FRONT   REAR
Often confused with deer but toes are wider, rounder and blunter and don't come to a point. Have dew claw that rests slightly outside print.

Reptile / Amphibian

Alligator

FRONT
REAR
Large feet with four toes on front prints and five toes on rear prints. Front are wide in heel, rear are longer, narrow and pointed heel.

Lizard

FRONT   REAR
Lightweight and don't leave much of a track. Might leave small scuff from feet and small tail drag.

Frog

FRONT   REAR
Have four bulbous toes in front and five in hind prints. Front toes point slightly inward producing a "K" shaped print, while rear toes slope upward and outward.

Other Common

Raccoon

FRONT
REAR
Five toes resembles hand of a baby. Front print smaller (1-3") with C-shaped heel pad. Rear print longer (1.5-4") heel pad.

Opossum

FRONT   REAR
Five fingers and human hand shape. Opposable thumbs on hind feet.

Rabbit
REAR

FRONT
Larger hind feet, smaller front feet. Hoppers producing a "Y" shaped track.

Skunk

FRONT
REAR
Five toes on their hind and front feet. Front and rear are approximately same size. Claws show up in many prints.

Otter

FRONT   REAR
Five toes and short claws give their prints a pointed look. Toes are partially webbed.

Armadillo
REAR

FRONT
Four long toe prints with sharp claw at tip. Front print show distinct "V" between middle toes.

Sketch / Notes

Sketch

_____
_____
_____
_____
_____
_____
_____
_____
_____
_____
_____

General

Date: _____   Location: _____

Environment: ◯ Mud   ◯ Snow   ◯ Soft Garden Soil   ◯ Sand

Time of Day: ◯ Morning   ◯ Midday   ◯ Evening   ◯ Time _____

Front Toes: ◯ Five   ◯ Four   ◯ Three   ◯ Two

Rear Toes: ◯ Five   ◯ Four   ◯ Three   ◯ Two

Track Symmetry: ◯ Symmetric   ◯ Asymmetric

Claws / Nails: ◯ Visible   ◯ Not Visible   Webbing: ◯ Yes   ◯ No

Surroundings: _____

Movement Pattern: ◯ Zig-Zaggler   ◯ Trot   ◯ Lope   ◯ Gallop

Notes: _____

Canine

Wolf

FRONT   REAR

Biggest in this group with a long (4") and wide print.

Coyote
FRONT   REAR

Slightly smaller than wolves with print more narrow (2.5 to 3.5").

Fox
FRONT   REAR

Smallest in the group with print (2 to 3") and fuzzy around edges.

Dog
FRONT   REAR

Similar to wolf/coyote with thicker nails.

Feline

Cougar / Mountain Lion

FRONT   REAR

Largest in the group (greater than 3"). Size of domestic dog.

Lynx

FRONT   REAR

Same as cougar but smaller in size and not as defined due to fur around paws.

Bobcat

FRONT   REAR

Smaller tracks (2"). Often confused with coyote or fox but lacks nails. Round shape.

House Cat

FRONT   REAR

Small (1 to 1.5"). Similar to domestic dog, meander when walking.

Bird

Crow
Standard bird track: 3 forward, 1 rear. Print 2-2.5".

Grouse
Small ground birds with only 3 forward toes. Print 2" long.

Turkey
Similar to grouse but much larger prints (4") long.

Duck
Webbing gives its print distinctive shape.

Bear

Black Bear

FRONT   REAR

Has short claws and its toes spread out in a curve over its foot pad. Generally going to be smaller than grizzly bear paw.

Grizzly Bear

FRONT   REAR

Has long claws that extend out further from their toes. Its toes also are held closer together, forming almost a straight line above the foot pad.

Rodent

Beaver

FRONT   REAR
Webbed hind feet with 5 toes (4.5-7"). Sometime 4-toed prints.

Porcupine

FRONT REAR
Usually only see pads in prints (1-2"). Pigeon-toed.

Muskrat

FRONT   REAR
Hand-like like raccoon but smaller (2.3").

Mouse

FRONT   REAR
Larger back feet (1.5 - 2"), smaller front feet (0.25-0.5").

Squirrel

FRONT   REAR
Larger back feet (1.5-2"), smaller front feet (1-1.5").

Hoof

Mountain Goat

FRONT   REAR
Have toes that spread when they step, creating a distinctive V shape at the top of their print.

Bighorn Sheep

FRONT   REAR
Similar to deer but with straighter edges and less pointed. More blocky and less shaped like a heart.

Wild Hog

FRONT   REAR
Often confused with deer but toes are wider, rounder and blunter and don't come to a point. Have a dew claw that rests slightly outside print.

Reptile / Amphibian

Alligator

FRONT

REAR
Large feet with four toes on front prints and five toes on rear prints. Front are wide in heel, rear are longer, narrow and pointed heel.

Lizard

FRONT   REAR
Lightweight and don't leave much of a track. Might leave small scuff from feet and small tail drag.

Frog

FRONT   REAR
Have four bulbous toes in front and five in hind prints. Front toes point slightly inward producing a "K" shaped print, while rear toes slope upward and outward.

Other Common

Raccoon

FRONT

REAR
Five toes resembles hand of a baby. Front print smaller (1-3") with C-shaped heel pad. Rear print longer (1.5-4") heel pad.

Opossum

FRONT   REAR
Five fingers and human hand shape. Opposable thumbs on hind feet.

Rabbit
REAR

FRONT
Larger hind feet, smaller front feet. Hoppers producing a "Y" shaped track.

Skunk

FRONT

REAR
Five toes on their hind and front feet. Front and rear are approximately same size. Claws show up in many prints.

Otter

FRONT   REAR
Five toes and short claws give their prints a pointed look. Toes are partially webbed.

Armadillo
REAR

FRONT
Four long toe prints with sharp claw at tip. Front print show distinct "V" between middle toes.

Sketch

Sketch / Notes

_____
_____
_____
_____
_____
_____
_____
_____
_____
_____
_____

General

Date: _____ Location: _____

Environment: ⬭ Mud ⬭ Snow ⬭ Soft Garden Soil ⬭ Sand

Time of Day: ⬭ Morning ⬭ Midday ⬭ Evening ⬭ Time _____

Front Toes: ⬭ Five ⬭ Four ⬭ Three ⬭ Two

Rear Toes: ⬭ Five ⬭ Four ⬭ Three ⬭ Two

Track Symmetry: ⬭ Symmetric ⬭ Asymmetric

Claws / Nails: ⬭ Visible ⬭ Not Visible   Webbing: ⬭ Yes ⬭ No

Surroundings: _____

Movement Pattern: ⬭ Zig-Zaggler ⬭ Trot ⬭ Lope ⬭ Gallop

Notes: _____

Canine

Wolf

FRONT   REAR

Biggest in this group with a long (4") and wide print.

Coyote
FRONT   REAR

Slightly smaller than wolves with print more narrow (2.5 to 3.5").

Fox
FRONT   REAR

Smallest in the group with print (2 to 3") and fuzzy around edges.

Dog
FRONT   REAR

Similar to wolf/coyote with thicker nails.

Feline

Cougar / Mountain Lion

FRONT   REAR

Largest in the group (greater than 3"). Size of domestic dog.

Lynx

FRONT   REAR

Same as cougar but smaller in size and not as defined due to fur around paws.

Bobcat

FRONT   REAR

Smaller tracks (2"). Often confused with coyote or fox but lacks nails. Round shape.

House Cat

FRONT   REAR

Small (1 to 1.5"). Similar to domestic dog, meander when walking.

Bird

Crow

Standard bird track: 3 forward, 1 rear. Print 2-2.5".

Grouse

Small ground birds with only 3 forward toes. Print 2" long.

Turkey

Similar to grouse but much larger prints (4") long.

Duck

Webbing gives its print distinctive shape.

Bear

Black Bear
FRONT   REAR

Has short claws and its toes spread out in a curve over its foot pad. Generally going to be smaller than grizzly bear paw.

Grizzly Bear

FRONT   REAR

Has long claws that extend out further from their toes. Its toes also are held closer together, forming almost a straight line above the foot pad.

Rodent

Beaver

FRONT   REAR
Webbed hind feet with 5 toes (4.5-7"). Sometime 4-toed prints.

Porcupine

FRONT   REAR
Usually only see pads in prints (1-2"). Pigeon-toed.

Muskrat

FRONT   REAR
Hand-like like raccoon but smaller (2.3").

Mouse

FRONT   REAR
Larger back feet (1.5 - 2"), smaller front feet (0.25-0.5").

Squirrel

FRONT   REAR
Larger back feet (1.5-2"), smaller front feet (1-1.5").

Hoof

Mountain Goat

FRONT   REAR
Have toes that spread when they step, creating a distinctive V shape at the top of their print.

Bighorn Sheep

FRONT   REAR
Similar to deer but with straighter edges and less pointed. More blocky and less shaped like a heart.

Wild Hog

FRONT   REAR
Often confused with deer but toes are wider, rounder and blunter and don't come to a point. Have dew claw that rests slightly outside print.

Reptile / Amphibian

Alligator

FRONT   REAR
Large feet with four toes on front prints and five toes on rear prints. Front are wide in heel, rear are longer, narrow and pointed heel.

Lizard

FRONT   REAR
Lightweight and don't leave much of a track. Might leave small scuff from feet and small tail drag.

Frog

FRONT   REAR
Have four bulbous toes in front and five in hind prints. Front toes point slightly inward producing a "K" shaped print, while rear toes slope upward and outward.

Other Common

Raccoon

FRONT   REAR
Five toes resembles hand of a baby. Front print smaller (1-3") with C-shaped heel pad. Rear print longer (1.5-4") heel pad.

Opossum

FRONT   REAR
Five fingers and human hand shape. Opposable thumbs on hind feet.

Rabbit
REAR
FRONT
Larger hind feet, smaller front feet. Hoppers producing a "Y" shaped track.

Skunk

FRONT   REAR
Five toes on their hind and front feet. Front and rear are approximately same size. Claws show up in many prints.

Otter

FRONT   REAR
Five toes and short claws give their prints a pointed look. Toes are partially webbed.

Armadillo

REAR
FRONT
Four long toe prints with sharp claw at tip. Front print show distinct "V" between middle toes.

Sketch

Sketch / Notes

General

Date: _____ Location: _____

Environment: ⬭ Mud ⬭ Snow ⬭ Soft Garden Soil ⬭ Sand

Time of Day: ⬭ Morning ⬭ Midday ⬭ Evening ⬭ Time_____

Front Toes: ⬭ Five ⬭ Four ⬭ Three ⬭ Two

Rear Toes: ⬭ Five ⬭ Four ⬭ Three ⬭ Two

Track Symmetry: ⬭ Symmetric ⬭ Asymmetric

Claws / Nails: ⬭ Visible ⬭ Not Visible   Webbing: ⬭ Yes ⬭ No

Surroundings: _____

Movement Pattern: ⬭ Zig-Zaggler ⬭ Trot ⬭ Lope ⬭ Gallop

Notes: _____

Canine

Wolf	Coyote	Fox	Dog
FRONT REAR	FRONT REAR	FRONT REAR	FRONT REAR
Biggest in this group with a long (4") and wide print.	Slightly smaller than wolves with print more narrow (2.5 to 3.5").	Smallest in the group with print (2 to 3") and fuzzy around edges.	Similar to wolf/coyote with thicker nails.

Feline

Cougar / Mountain Lion	Lynx	Bobcat	House Cat
FRONT REAR	FRONT REAR	FRONT REAR	FRONT REAR
Largest in the group (greater than 3"). Size of domestic dog.	Same as cougar but smaller in size and not as defined due to fur around paws.	Smaller tracks (2"). Often confused with coyote or fox but lacks nails. Round shape.	Small (1 to 1.5"). Similar to domestic dog, meander when walking.

Bird

Crow	Grouse	Turkey	Duck
Standard bird track: 3 forward, 1 rear. Print 2-2.5".	Small ground birds with only 3 forward toes. Print 2" long.	Similar to grouse but much larger prints (4") long.	Webbing gives its print distinctive shape.

Bear

Black Bear

FRONT   REAR

Has short claws and its toes spread out in a curve over its foot pad. Generally going to be smaller than grizzly bear paw.

Grizzly Bear

FRONT   REAR

Has long claws that extend out further from their toes. Its toes also are held closer together, forming almost a straight line above the foot pad.

Rodent

Beaver

FRONT   REAR
Webbed hind feet with 5 toes (4.5-7"). Sometime 4-toed prints.

Porcupine

FRONT   REAR
Usually only see pads in prints (1-2"). Pigeon-toed.

Muskrat

FRONT   REAR
Hand-like like raccoon but smaller (2.3").

Mouse
FRONT   REAR
Larger back feet (1.5 - 2"), smaller front feet (0.25-0.5").

Squirrel

FRONT   REAR
Larger back feet (1.5-2"), smaller front feet (1-1.5").

Mountain Goat

FRONT   REAR
Have toes that spread when they step, creating a distinctive V shape at the top of their print.

Bighorn Sheep

FRONT   REAR
Similar to deer but with straighter edges and less pointed. More blocky and less shaped like a heart.

Wild Hog

FRONT   REAR
Often confused with deer but toes are wider, rounder and blunter and don't come to a point. Have dew claw that rests slightly outside print.

Alligator

FRONT
REAR
Large feet with four toes on front prints and five toes on rear prints. Front are wide in heel, rear are longer, narrow and pointed heel.

Lizard

FRONT   REAR
Lightweight and don't leave much of a track. Might leave small scuff from feet and small tail drag.

Frog

FRONT   REAR
Have four bulbous toes in front and five in hind prints. Front toes point slightly inward producing a "K" shaped print, while rear toes slope upward and outward.

Raccoon

FRONT
REAR
Five toes resembles hand of a baby. Front print smaller (1-3") with C-shaped heel pad. Rear print longer (1.5-4') heel pad.

Opossum

FRONT   REAR
Five fingers and human hand shape. Opposable thumbs on hind feet .

Rabbit
REAR
FRONT
Larger hind feet, smaller front feet. Hoppers producing a "Y" shaped track.

Skunk

FRONT
REAR
Five toes on their hind and front feet. Front and rear are approximately same size. Claws show up in many prints.

Otter

FRONT   REAR
Five toes and short claws give their prints a pointed look. Toes are partially webbed.

Armadillo
REAR

FRONT
Four long toe prints with sharp claw at tip. Front print show distinct "V" between middle toes.

Sketch

_____
_____
_____
_____
_____
_____
_____
_____
_____
_____
_____

General

Date: _____ Location: _____

Environment: ◯ Mud ◯ Snow ◯ Soft Garden Soil ◯ Sand

Time of Day: ◯ Morning ◯ Midday ◯ Evening ◯ Time _____

Front Toes: ◯ Five ◯ Four ◯ Three ◯ Two

Rear Toes: ◯ Five ◯ Four ◯ Three ◯ Two

Track Symmetry: ◯ Symmetric ◯ Asymmetric

Claws / Nails: ◯ Visible ◯ Not Visible   Webbing: ◯ Yes ◯ No

Surroundings: _____

Movement Pattern: ◯ Zig-Zaggler ◯ Trot ◯ Lope ◯ Gallop

Notes: _____

Canine

Wolf
FRONT REAR

Biggest in this group with a long (4") and wide print.

Coyote
FRONT REAR

Slightly smaller than wolves with print more narrow (2.5 to 3.5").

Fox
FRONT REAR

Smallest in the group with print (2 to 3") and fuzzy around edges.

Dog
FRONT REAR

Similar to wolf/coyote with thicker nails.

Feline

Cougar / Mountain Lion
FRONT REAR

Largest in the group (greater than 3"). Size of domestic dog.

Lynx
FRONT REAR

Same as cougar but smaller in size and not as defined due to fur around paws.

Bobcat
FRONT REAR

Smaller tracks (2"). Often confused with coyote or fox but lacks nails. Round shape.

House Cat
FRONT REAR

Small (1 to 1.5"). Similar to domestic dog, meander when walking.

Bird

Crow

Standard bird track: 3 forward, 1 rear. Print 2-2.5".

Grouse

Small ground birds with only 3 forward toes. Print 2" long.

Turkey

Similar to grouse but much larger prints (4") long.

Duck

Webbing gives its print distinctive shape.

Bear

Black Bear

FRONT REAR

Has short claws and its toes spread out in a curve over its foot pad. Generally going to be smaller than grizzly bear paw.

Grizzly Bear
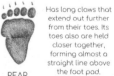
FRONT REAR

Has long claws that extend out further from their toes. Its toes also are held closer together, forming almost a straight line above the foot pad.

Rodent

Beaver

FRONT   REAR
Webbed hind feet with 5 toes (4.5-7"). Sometime 4-toed prints.

Porcupine

FRONT   REAR
Usually only see pads in prints (1-2"). Pigeon-toed.

Muskrat

FRONT   REAR
Hand-like like raccoon but smaller (2.3").

Mouse

FRONT   REAR
Larger back feet (1.5 - 2"), smaller front feet (0.25-0.5").

Squirrel

FRONT   REAR
Larger back feet (1.5-2"), smaller front feet (1-1.5").

Hoof

Mountain Goat

FRONT   REAR
Have toes that spread when they step, creating a distinctive V shape at the top of their print.

Bighorn Sheep

FRONT   REAR
Similar to deer but with straighter edges and less pointed. More blocky and less shaped like a heart.

Wild Hog

FRONT   REAR
Often confused with deer but toes are wider, rounder and blunter and don't come to a point. Have dew claw that rests slightly outside print.

Reptile / Amphibian

Alligator

FRONT
REAR
Large feet with four toes on front prints and five toes on rear prints. Front are wide in heel, rear are longer, narrow and pointed heel.

Lizard

FRONT   REAR
Lightweight and don't leave much of a track. Might leave small scuff from feet and small tail drag.

Frog
FRONT   REAR
Have four bulbous toes in front and five in hind prints. Front toes point slightly inward producing a "K" shaped print, while rear toes slope upward and outward.

Other Common

Raccoon

FRONT
REAR
Five toes resembles hand of a baby. Front print smaller (1-3") with C-shaped heel pad. Rear print longer (1.5-4") heel pad.

Opossum

FRONT   REAR
Five fingers and human hand shape. Opposable thumbs on hind feet .

Rabbit
REAR

FRONT
Larger hind feet, smaller front feet. Hoppers producing a "Y" shaped track.

Skunk

FRONT
REAR
Five toes on their hind and front feet. Front and rear are approximately same size. Claws show up in many prints.

Otter

FRONT   REAR
Five toes and short claws give their prints a pointed look. Toes are partially webbed.

Armadillo
REAR

FRONT
Four long toe prints with sharp claw at tip. Front print show distinct "V" between middle toes.

Sketch

_____
_____
_____
_____
_____
_____
_____
_____
_____
_____
_____

Sketch / Notes

General

Date: _____   Location: _____

Environment: ◯ Mud   ◯ Snow   ◯ Soft Garden Soil   ◯ Sand

Time of Day: ◯ Morning   ◯ Midday   ◯ Evening   ◯ Time_____

Front Toes: ◯ Five   ◯ Four   ◯ Three   ◯ Two

Rear Toes: ◯ Five   ◯ Four   ◯ Three   ◯ Two

Track Symmetry: ◯ Symmetric   ◯ Asymmetric

Claws / Nails: ◯ Visible   ◯ Not Visible   Webbing: ◯ Yes   ◯ No

Surroundings: _____

Movement Pattern: ◯ Zig-Zaggler   ◯ Trot   ◯ Lope   ◯ Gallop

Notes: _____

Canine

Wolf

FRONT   REAR

Biggest in this group with a long (4") and wide print.

Coyote
FRONT   REAR

Slightly smaller than wolves with print more narrow (2.5 to 3.5").

Fox
FRONT   REAR

Smallest in the group with print (2 to 3") and fuzzy around edges.

Dog
FRONT   REAR

Similar to wolf/coyote with thicker nails.

Feline

Cougar / Mountain Lion
FRONT   REAR

Largest in the group (greater than 3"). Size of domestic dog.

Lynx
FRONT   REAR

Same as cougar but smaller in size and not as defined due to fur around paws.

Bobcat
FRONT   REAR

Smaller tracks (2"). Often confused with coyote or fox but lacks nails. Round shape.

House Cat
FRONT   REAR

Small (1 to 1.5"). Similar to domestic dog, meander when walking.

Bird

Crow

Standard bird track: 3 forward, 1 rear. Print 2-2.5".

Grouse

Small ground birds with only 3 forward toes. Print 2" long.

Turkey

Similar to grouse but much larger prints (4") long.

Duck

Webbing gives its print distinctive shape.

Bear

Black Bear

FRONT   REAR

Has short claws and its toes spread out in a curve over its foot pad. Generally going to be smaller than grizzly bear paw.

Grizzly Bear

FRONT   REAR

Has long claws that extend out further from their toes. Its toes also are held closer together, forming almost a straight line above the foot pad.

Rodent

Beaver

FRONT   REAR
Webbed hind feet with 5 toes (4.5-7). Sometime 4-toed prints.

Porcupine

FRONT   REAR
Usually only see pads in prints (1-2"). Pigeon-toed.

Muskrat

FRONT   REAR
Hand-like like raccoon but smaller (2.3").

Mouse

FRONT   REAR
Larger back feet (1.5 - 2"), smaller front feet (0.25-0.5").

Squirrel

FRONT   REAR
Larger back feet (1.5-2"), smaller front feet (1-1.5").

Hoof

Mountain Goat

FRONT   REAR
Have toes that spread when they step, creating a distinctive V shape at the top of their print.

Bighorn Sheep

FRONT   REAR
Similar to deer but with straighter edges and less pointed. More blocky and less shaped like a heart.

Wild Hog

FRONT   REAR
Often confused with deer but toes are wider, rounder and blunter and don't come to a point. Have dew claw that rests slightly outside print.

Reptile / Amphibian

Alligator

FRONT
REAR
Large feet with four toes on front prints and five toes on rear prints. Front are wide in heel, rear are longer, narrow and pointed heel.

Lizard

FRONT   REAR
Lightweight and don't leave much of a track. Might leave small scuff from feet and small tail drag.

Frog

FRONT   REAR
Have four bulbous toes in front and five in hind prints. Front toes point slightly inward producing a "K" shaped print, while rear toes slope upward and outward.

Other Common

Raccoon

FRONT
REAR
Five toes resembles hand of a baby. Front print smaller (1-3") with C-shaped heel pad. Rear print longer (1.5-4") heel pad.

Opossum

FRONT   REAR
Five fingers and human hand shape. Opposable thumbs on hind feet.

Rabbit
REAR
FRONT
Larger hind feet, smaller front feet. Hoppers producing a "Y" shaped track.

Skunk

FRONT   REAR
Five toes on their hind and front feet. Front and rear are approximately same size. Claws show up in many prints.

Otter

FRONT   REAR
Five toes and short claws give their prints a pointed look. Toes are partially webbed.

Armadillo
REAR
FRONT
Four long toe prints with sharp claw at tip. Front print show distinct "V" between middle toes.

Sketch / Notes

Sketch

_____
_____
_____
_____
_____
_____
_____
_____
_____
_____

General

Date: _____   Location: _____

Environment: ◯ Mud   ◯ Snow   ◯ Soft Garden Soil   ◯ Sand

Time of Day: ◯ Morning   ◯ Midday   ◯ Evening   ◯ Time _____

Front Toes: ◯ Five   ◯ Four   ◯ Three   ◯ Two

Rear Toes: ◯ Five   ◯ Four   ◯ Three   ◯ Two

Track Symmetry: ◯ Symmetric   ◯ Asymmetric

Claws / Nails: ◯ Visible   ◯ Not Visible   Webbing: ◯ Yes   ◯ No

Surroundings: _____

Movement Pattern: ◯ Zig-Zaggler   ◯ Trot   ◯ Lope   ◯ Gallop

Notes: _____

Canine

Wolf	Coyote	Fox	Dog

FRONT REAR   FRONT REAR   FRONT REAR   FRONT REAR

| Biggest in this group with a long (4") and wide print. | Slightly smaller than wolves with print more narrow (2.5 to 3.5"). | Smallest in the group with print (2 to 3") and fuzzy around edges. | Similar to wolf/coyote with thicker nails. |

Feline

Cougar / Mountain Lion	Lynx	Bobcat	House Cat

FRONT REAR   FRONT REAR   FRONT REAR   FRONT REAR

| Largest in the group (greater than 3"). Size of domestic dog. | Same as cougar but smaller in size and not as defined due to fur around paws. | Smaller tracks (2"). Often confused with coyote or fox but lacks nails. Round shape. | Small (1 to 1.5"). Similar to domestic dog, meander when walking. |

Bird

Crow	Grouse	Turkey	Duck

| Standard bird track: 3 forward, 1 rear. Print 2-2.5". | Small ground birds with only 3 forward toes. Print 2" long. | Similar to grouse but much larger prints (4") long. | Webbing gives its print distinctive shape. |

Bear

Black Bear

FRONT   REAR

Has short claws and its toes spread out in a curve over its foot pad. Generally going to be smaller than grizzly bear paw.

Grizzly Bear

FRONT   REAR

Has long claws that extend out further from their toes. Its toes also are held closer together, forming almost a straight line above the foot pad.

Rodent

Beaver

FRONT   REAR

Webbed hind feet with 5 toes (4.5-7"). Sometime 4-toed prints.

Porcupine

FRONT   REAR

Usually only see pads in prints (1-2"). Pigeon-toed.

Muskrat

FRONT   REAR

Hand-like like raccoon but smaller (2.3").

Mouse

FRONT   REAR

Larger back feet (1.5 - 2"), smaller front feet (0.25-0.5").

Squirrel

FRONT   REAR

Larger back feet (1.5-2"), smaller front feet (1-1.5").

Hoof

Mountain Goat

FRONT   REAR

Have toes that spread when they step, creating a distinctive V shape at the top of their print.

Bighorn Sheep

FRONT   REAR

Similar to deer but with straighter edges and less pointed. More blocky and less shaped like a heart.

Wild Hog

FRONT   REAR

Often confused with deer but toes are wider, rounder and blunter and don't come to a point. Have dew claw that rests slightly outside print.

Reptile / Amphibian

Alligator

FRONT

REAR

Large feet with four toes on front prints and five toes on rear prints. Front are wide in heel, rear are longer, narrow and pointed heel.

Lizard

FRONT   REAR

Lightweight and don't leave much of a track. Might leave small scuff from feet and small tail drag.

Frog

FRONT   REAR

Have four bulbous toes in front and five in hind prints. Front toes point slightly inward producing a "K" shaped print, while rear toes slope upward and outward.

Other Common

Raccoon

FRONT

REAR

Five toes resembles hand of a baby. Front print smaller (1-3") with C-shaped heel pad. Rear print longer (1.5-4") heel pad.

Opossum

FRONT   REAR

Five fingers and human hand shape. Opposable thumbs on hind feet.

Rabbit
REAR

FRONT

Larger hind feet, smaller front feet. Hoppers producing a "Y" shaped track.

Skunk

FRONT   REAR

Five toes on their hind and front feet. Front and rear are approximately same size. Claws show up in many prints.

Otter

FRONT   REAR

Five toes and short claws give their prints a pointed look. Toes are partially webbed.

Armadillo
REAR

FRONT

Four long toe prints with sharp claw at tip. Front print show distinct "V" between middle toes.

Sketch / Notes

Sketch

_____
_____
_____
_____
_____
_____
_____
_____
_____
_____
_____

General

Date: _____ Location: _____

Environment: ⃝ Mud   ⃝ Snow   ⃝ Soft Garden Soil   ⃝ Sand

Time of Day: ⃝ Morning   ⃝ Midday   ⃝ Evening   ⃝ Time _____

Front Toes: ⃝ Five   ⃝ Four   ⃝ Three   ⃝ Two

Rear Toes: ⃝ Five   ⃝ Four   ⃝ Three   ⃝ Two

Track Symmetry: ⃝ Symmetric   ⃝ Asymmetric

Claws / Nails: ⃝ Visible   ⃝ Not Visible   Webbing: ⃝ Yes   ⃝ No

Surroundings: _____

Movement Pattern: ⃝ Zig-Zaggler   ⃝ Trot   ⃝ Lope   ⃝ Gallop

Notes: _____

Canine

Wolf	Coyote	Fox	Dog

FRONT REAR | FRONT REAR | FRONT REAR | FRONT REAR

Biggest in this group with a long (4") and wide print.

Slightly smaller than wolves with print more narrow (2.5 to 3.5").

Smallest in the group with print (2 to 3") and fuzzy around edges.

Similar to wolf/coyote with thicker nails.

Feline

Cougar / Mountain Lion	Lynx	Bobcat	House Cat

FRONT REAR | FRONT REAR | FRONT REAR | FRONT REAR

Largest in the group (greater than 3"). Size of domestic dog.

Same as cougar but smaller in size and not as defined due to fur around paws.

Smaller tracks (2"). Often confused with coyote or fox but lacks nails. Round shape.

Small (1 to 1.5"). Similar to domestic dog, meander when walking.

Bird

Crow	Grouse	Turkey	Duck

Standard bird track: 3 forward, 1 rear. Print 2-2.5".

Small ground birds with only 3 forward toes. Print 2" long.

Similar to grouse but much larger prints (4") long.

Webbing gives its print distinctive shape.

Bear

Black Bear

FRONT REAR

Has short claws and its toes spread out in a curve over its foot pad. Generally going to be smaller than grizzly bear paw.

Grizzly Bear

FRONT REAR

Has long claws that extend out further from their toes. Its toes also are held closer together, forming almost a straight line above the foot pad.

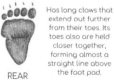

Rodent

Beaver

FRONT   REAR
Webbed hind feet with 5 toes (4.5-7"). Sometime 4-toed prints.

Porcupine

FRONT   REAR
Usually only see pads in prints (1-2"). Pigeon-toed.

Muskrat

FRONT   REAR
Hand-like like raccoon but smaller (2.3").

Mouse

FRONT   REAR
Larger back feet (1.5 - 2"), smaller front feet (0.25-0.5").

Squirrel

FRONT   REAR
Larger back feet (1.5-2"), smaller front feet (1-1.5").

Hoof

Mountain Goat

FRONT   REAR
Have toes that spread when they step, creating a distinctive V shape at the top of their print.

Bighorn Sheep

FRONT   REAR
Similar to deer but with straighter edges and less pointed. More blocky and less shaped like a heart.

Wild Hog

FRONT   REAR
Often confused with deer but toes are wider, rounder and blunter and don't come to a point. Have dew claw that rests slightly outside print.

Reptile / Amphibian

Alligator

FRONT
REAR
Large feet with four toes on front prints and five toes on rear prints. Front are wide in heel, rear are longer, narrow and pointed heel.

Lizard

FRONT   REAR
Lightweight and don't leave much of a track. Might leave small scuff from feet and small tail drag.

Frog

FRONT   REAR
Have four bulbous toes in front and five in hind prints. Front toes point slightly inward producing a "K" shaped print, while rear toes slope upward and outward.

Other Common

Raccoon

FRONT
REAR
Five toes resembles hand of a baby. Front print smaller (1-3") with C-shaped heel pad. Rear print longer (1.5-4") heel pad.

Opossum

FRONT   REAR
Five fingers and human hand shape. Opposable thumbs on hind feet .

Rabbit
REAR

FRONT
Larger hind feet, smaller front feet. Hoppers producing a "Y" shaped track.

Skunk

FRONT
REAR
Five toes on their hind and front feet. Front and rear are approximately same size. Claws show up in many prints.

Otter

FRONT   REAR
Five toes and short claws give their prints a pointed look. Toes are partially webbed.

Armadillo
REAR

FRONT
Four long toe prints with sharp claw at tip. Front print show distinct "V" between middle toes.

Sketch / Notes

Sketch

_____
_____
_____
_____
_____
_____
_____
_____
_____
_____
_____

General

Date: _____ Location: _____

Environment: ◯ Mud ◯ Snow ◯ Soft Garden Soil ◯ Sand

Time of Day: ◯ Morning ◯ Midday ◯ Evening ◯ Time_____

Front Toes: ◯ Five ◯ Four ◯ Three ◯ Two

Rear Toes: ◯ Five ◯ Four ◯ Three ◯ Two

Track Symmetry: ◯ Symmetric ◯ Asymmetric

Claws / Nails: ◯ Visible ◯ Not Visible Webbing: ◯ Yes ◯ No

Surroundings: _____

Movement Pattern: ◯ Zig-Zaggler ◯ Trot ◯ Lope ◯ Gallop

Notes: _____

Canine

Wolf	Coyote	Fox	Dog

FRONT REAR   FRONT REAR   FRONT REAR   FRONT REAR

| Biggest in this group with a long (4") and wide print. | Slightly smaller than wolves with print more narrow (2.5 to 3.5"). | Smallest in the group with print (2 to 3") and fuzzy around edges. | Similar to wolf/coyote with thicker nails. |

Feline

Cougar / Mountain Lion	Lynx	Bobcat	House Cat

FRONT REAR   FRONT REAR   FRONT REAR   FRONT REAR

| Largest in the group (greater than 3"). Size of domestic dog. | Same as cougar but smaller in size and not as defined due to fur around paws. | Smaller tracks (2"). Often confused with coyote or fox but lacks nails. Round shape. | Small (1 to 1.5"). Similar to domestic dog, meander when walking. |

Bird

Crow	Grouse	Turkey	Duck

| Standard bird track: 3 forward, 1 rear. Print 2-2.5". | Small ground birds with only 3 forward toes. Print 2" long. | Similar to grouse but much larger prints (4") long. | Webbing gives its print distinctive shape. |

Bear

Black Bear

FRONT REAR

Has short claws and its toes spread out in a curve over its foot pad. Generally going to be smaller than grizzly bear paw.

Grizzly Bear

FRONT REAR

Has long claws that extend out further from their toes. Its toes also are held closer together, forming almost a straight line above the foot pad.

Rodent

Beaver

FRONT   REAR
Webbed hind feet with 5 toes (4.5-7"). Sometime 4-toed prints.

Porcupine

FRONT   REAR
Usually only see pads in prints (1-2"). Pigeon-toed.

Muskrat

FRONT   REAR
Hand-like like raccoon but smaller (2.3").

Mouse
FRONT   REAR
Larger back feet (1.5 - 2"), smaller front feet (0.25-0.5").

Squirrel

FRONT   REAR
Larger back feet (1.5-2"), smaller front feet (1-1.5").

Hoof

Mountain Goat

FRONT   REAR
Have toes that spread when they step, creating a distinctive V shape at the top of their print.

Bighorn Sheep
FRONT   REAR
Similar to deer but with straighter edges and less pointed. More blocky and less shaped like a heart.

Wild Hog

FRONT   REAR
Often confused with deer but toes are wider, rounder and blunter and don't come to a point. Have dew claw that rests slightly outside print.

Reptile / Amphibian

Alligator

FRONT

REAR

Large feet with four toes on front prints and five toes on rear prints. Front are wide in heel, rear are longer, narrow and pointed heel.

Lizard

FRONT   REAR
Lightweight and don't leave much of a track. Might leave small scuff from feet and small tail drag.

Frog

FRONT   REAR
Have four bulbous toes in front and five in hind prints. Front toes point slightly inward producing a "K" shaped print, while rear toes slope upward and outward.

Other Common

Raccoon

FRONT

REAR

Five toes resembles hand of a baby. Front print smaller (1-3") with C-shaped heel pad. Rear print longer (1.5-4") heel pad.

Opossum

FRONT   REAR
Five fingers and human hand shape. Opposable thumbs on hind feet .

Rabbit
REAR

FRONT
Larger hind feet, smaller front feet. Hoppers producing a "Y" shaped track.

Skunk

FRONT

REAR

Five toes on their hind and front feet. Front and rear are approximately same size. Claws show up in many prints.

Otter

FRONT   REAR
Five toes and short claws give their prints a pointed look. Toes are partially webbed.

Armadillo
REAR

FRONT

Four long toe prints with sharp claw at tip. Front print show distinct "V" between middle toes.

Sketch / Notes

Sketch

General

Date: _____ Location: _____

Environment: ◯ Mud ◯ Snow ◯ Soft Garden Soil ◯ Sand

Time of Day: ◯ Morning ◯ Midday ◯ Evening ◯ Time _____

Front Toes: ◯ Five ◯ Four ◯ Three ◯ Two

Rear Toes: ◯ Five ◯ Four ◯ Three ◯ Two

Track Symmetry: ◯ Symmetric ◯ Asymmetric

Claws / Nails: ◯ Visible ◯ Not Visible   Webbing: ◯ Yes ◯ No

Surroundings: _____

Movement Pattern: ◯ Zig-Zaggler   ◯ Trot   ◯ Lope   ◯ Gallop

Notes: _____

Canine

Wolf

FRONT   REAR

Biggest in this group with a long (4") and wide print.

Coyote
FRONT   REAR

Slightly smaller than wolves with print more narrow (2.5 to 3.5").

Fox

FRONT   REAR

Smallest in the group with print (2 to 3") and fuzzy around edges.

Dog

FRONT   REAR

Similar to wolf/coyote with thicker nails.

Feline

Cougar / Mountain Lion

FRONT   REAR

Largest in the group (greater than 3"). Size of domestic dog.

Lynx

FRONT   REAR

Same as cougar but smaller in size and not as defined due to fur around paws.

Bobcat

FRONT   REAR

Smaller tracks (2"). Often confused with coyote or fox but lacks nails. Round shape.

House Cat

FRONT   REAR

Small (1 to 1.5"). Similar to domestic dog, meander when walking.

Bird

Crow
FRONT   REAR

Standard bird track: 3 forward, 1 rear. Print 2-2.5".

Grouse

Small ground birds with only 3 forward toes. Print 2" long.

Turkey

Similar to grouse but much larger prints (4") long.

Duck

Webbing gives its print distinctive shape.

Bear

Black Bear

FRONT   REAR

Has short claws and its toes spread out in a curve over its foot pad. Generally going to be smaller than grizzly bear paw.

Grizzly Bear

FRONT   REAR

Has long claws that extend out further from their toes. Its toes also are held closer together, forming almost a straight line above the foot pad.

Rodent

Beaver

FRONT REAR
Webbed hind feet with 5 toes (4.5-7"). Sometime 4-toed prints.

Porcupine

FRONT REAR
Usually only see pads in prints (1-2"). Pigeon-toed.

Muskrat

FRONT REAR
Hand-like like raccoon but smaller (2.3").

Mouse

FRONT REAR
Larger back feet (1.5 - 2"), smaller front feet (0.25-0.5").

Squirrel

FRONT REAR
Larger back feet (1.5-2"), smaller front feet (1-1.5").

Hoof

Mountain Goat

FRONT REAR
Have toes that spread when they step, creating a distinctive V shape at the top of their print.

Bighorn Sheep
FRONT REAR
Similar to deer but with straighter edges and less pointed. More blocky and less shaped like a heart.

Wild Hog

FRONT REAR
Often confused with deer but toes are wider, rounder and blunter and don't come to a point. Have dew claw that rests slightly outside print.

Reptile / Amphibian

Alligator

FRONT
REAR
Large feet with four toes on front prints and five toes on rear prints. Front are wide in heel, rear are longer, narrow and pointed heel.

Lizard

FRONT REAR
Lightweight and don't leave much of a track. Might leave small scuff from feet and small tail drag.

Frog

FRONT REAR
Have four bulbous toes in front and five in hind prints. Front toes point slightly inward producing a "K" shaped print, while rear toes slope upward and outward.

Other Common

Raccoon

FRONT
REAR
Five toes resembles hand of a baby. Front print smaller (1-3") with C-shaped heel pad. Rear print longer (1.5-4") heel pad.

Opossum

FRONT REAR
Five fingers and human hand shape. Opposable thumbs on hind feet .

Rabbit
REAR

FRONT
Larger hind feet, smaller front feet. Hoppers producing a "Y" shaped track.

Skunk

FRONT
REAR
Five toes on their hind and front feet. Front and rear are approximately same size. Claws show up in many prints.

Otter

FRONT REAR
Five toes and short claws give their prints a pointed look. Toes are partially webbed.

Armadillo
REAR

FRONT
Four long toe prints with sharp claw at tip. Front print show distinct "V" between middle toes.

Sketch

Sketch / Notes

General

Date: _____   Location: _____

Environment: ◯ Mud   ◯ Snow   ◯ Soft Garden Soil   ◯ Sand

Time of Day: ◯ Morning   ◯ Midday   ◯ Evening   ◯ Time _____

Front Toes: ◯ Five   ◯ Four   ◯ Three   ◯ Two

Rear Toes: ◯ Five   ◯ Four   ◯ Three   ◯ Two

Track Symmetry: ◯ Symmetric   ◯ Asymmetric

Claws / Nails: ◯ Visible   ◯ Not Visible   Webbing: ◯ Yes   ◯ No

Surroundings: _____

Movement Pattern: ◯ Zig-Zaggler   ◯ Trot   ◯ Lope   ◯ Gallop

Notes: _____

Canine

Wolf

FRONT   REAR

Biggest in this group with a long (4") and wide print.

Coyote

FRONT   REAR

Slightly smaller than wolves with print more narrow (2.5 to 3.5").

Fox

FRONT   REAR

Smallest in the group with print (2 to 3") and fuzzy around edges.

Dog

FRONT   REAR

Similar to wolf/coyote with thicker nails.

Feline

Cougar / Mountain Lion

FRONT   REAR

Largest in the group (greater than 3"). Size of domestic dog.

Lynx

FRONT   REAR

Same as cougar but smaller in size and not as defined due to fur around paws.

Bobcat

FRONT   REAR

Smaller tracks (2"). Often confused with coyote or fox but lacks nails. Round shape.

House Cat

FRONT   REAR

Small (1 to 1.5"). Similar to domestic dog, meander when walking.

Bird

Crow

Standard bird track: 3 forward, 1 rear. Print 2-2.5".

Grouse

Small ground birds with only 3 forward toes. Print 2" long.

Turkey

Similar to grouse but much larger prints (4") long.

Duck

Webbing gives its print distinctive shape.

Bear

Black Bear

FRONT   REAR

Has short claws and its toes spread out in a curve over its foot pad. Generally going to be smaller than grizzly bear paw.

Grizzly Bear
FRONT   REAR

Has long claws that extend out further from their toes. Its toes also are held closer together, forming almost a straight line above the foot pad.

Rodent

Beaver

FRONT   REAR
Webbed hind feet with 5 toes (4.5-7"). Sometime 4-toed prints.

Porcupine

FRONT   REAR
Usually only see pads in prints (1-2"). Pigeon-toed.

Muskrat

FRONT   REAR
Hand-like like raccoon but smaller (2.3").

Mouse

FRONT   REAR
Larger back feet (1.5 - 2"), smaller front feet (0.25-0.5").

Squirrel
FRONT   REAR
Larger back feet (1.5-2"), smaller front feet (1-1.5").

Hoof

Mountain Goat

FRONT   REAR
Have toes that spread when they step, creating a distinctive V shape at the top of their print.

Bighorn Sheep

FRONT   REAR
Similar to deer but with straighter edges and less pointed. More blocky and less shaped like a heart.

Wild Hog

FRONT   REAR
Often confused with deer but toes are wider, rounder and blunter and don't come to a point. Have dew claw that rests slightly outside print.

Reptile / Amphibian

Alligator

FRONT
REAR
Large feet with four toes on front prints and five toes on rear prints. Front are wide in heel, rear are longer, narrow and pointed heel.

Lizard

FRONT   REAR
Lightweight and don't leave much of a track. Might leave small scuff from feet and small tail drag.

Frog

FRONT   REAR
Have four bulbous toes in front and five in hind prints. Front toes point slightly inward producing a "K" shaped print, while rear toes slope upward and outward.

Other Common

Raccoon

FRONT
REAR
Five toes resembles hand of a baby. Front print smaller (1-3") with C-shaped heel pad. Rear print longer (1.5-4") heel pad.

Opossum

FRONT   REAR
Five fingers and human hand shape. Opposable thumbs on hind feet .

Rabbit

REAR
FRONT
Larger hind feet, smaller front feet. Hoppers producing a "Y" shaped track.

Skunk

FRONT
REAR
Five toes on their hind and front feet. Front and rear are approximately same size. Claws show up in many prints.

Otter

FRONT   REAR
Five toes and short claws give their prints a pointed look. Toes are partially webbed.

Armadillo

REAR
FRONT
Four long toe prints with sharp claw at tip. Front print show distinct "V" between middle toes.

Sketch

Sketch / Notes

_____
_____
_____
_____
_____
_____
_____
_____
_____
_____
_____

General

Date: _____   Location: _____

Environment: ○ Mud   ○ Snow   ○ Soft Garden Soil   ○ Sand

Time of Day: ○ Morning   ○ Midday   ○ Evening   ○ Time _____

Front Toes: ○ Five   ○ Four   ○ Three   ○ Two

Rear Toes: ○ Five   ○ Four   ○ Three   ○ Two

Track Symmetry: ○ Symmetric   ○ Asymmetric

Claws / Nails: ○ Visible   ○ Not Visible   Webbing: ○ Yes   ○ No

Surroundings: _____

Movement Pattern: ○ Zig-Zaggler   ○ Trot   ○ Lope   ○ Gallop

Notes: _____

Canine

Wolf

FRONT   REAR

Biggest in this group with a long (4") and wide print.

Coyote
FRONT   REAR

Slightly smaller than wolves with print more narrow (2.5 to 3.5").

Fox
FRONT   REAR

Smallest in the group with print (2 to 3") and fuzzy around edges.

Dog
FRONT   REAR

Similar to wolf/coyote with thicker nails.

Feline

Cougar / Mountain Lion
FRONT   REAR

Largest in the group (greater than 3"). Size of domestic dog.

Lynx
FRONT   REAR

Same as cougar but smaller in size and not as defined due to fur around paws.

Bobcat
FRONT   REAR

Smaller tracks (2"). Often confused with coyote or fox but lacks nails. Round shape.

House Cat
FRONT   REAR

Small (1 to 1.5"). Similar to domestic dog, meander when walking.

Bird

Crow
Standard bird track: 3 forward, 1 rear. Print 2-2.5".

Grouse
Small ground birds with only 3 forward toes. Print 2" long.

Turkey
Similar to grouse but much larger prints (4") long.

Duck
Webbing gives its print distinctive shape.

Bear

Black Bear
FRONT   REAR

Has short claws and its toes spread out in a curve over its foot pad. Generally going to be smaller than grizzly bear paw.

Grizzly Bear
FRONT   REAR

Has long claws that extend out further from their toes. Its toes also are held closer together, forming almost a straight line above the foot pad.

Beaver

FRONT   REAR

Webbed hind feet with 5 toes (4.5-7"). Sometime 4-toed prints.

Porcupine

FRONT   REAR

Usually only see pads in prints (1-2"). Pigeon-toed.

Muskrat

FRONT   REAR

Hand-like like raccoon but smaller (2.3").

Mouse

FRONT   REAR

Larger back feet (1.5 - 2"), smaller front feet (0.25-0.5").

Squirrel

FRONT   REAR

Larger back feet (1.5-2"), smaller front feet (1-1.5").

Mountain Goat

FRONT   REAR

Have toes that spread when they step, creating a distinctive V shape at the top of their print.

Bighorn Sheep

FRONT   REAR

Similar to deer but with straighter edges and less pointed. More blocky and less shaped like a heart.

Wild Hog

FRONT   REAR

Often confused with deer but toes are wider, rounder and blunter and don't come to a point. Have dew claw that rests slightly outside print.

Alligator

FRONT

REAR

Large feet with four toes on front prints and five toes on rear prints. Front are wide in heel, rear are longer, narrow and pointed heel.

Lizard

FRONT   REAR

Lightweight and don't leave much of a track. Might leave small scuff from feet and small tail drag.

Frog

FRONT   REAR

Have four bulbous toes in front and five in hind prints. Front toes point slightly inward producing a "K" shaped print, while rear toes slope upward and outward.

Raccoon

FRONT

REAR

Five toes resembles hand of a baby. Front print smaller (1-3") with C-shaped heel pad. Rear print longer (1.5-4") heel pad.

Opossum

FRONT   REAR

Five fingers and human hand shape. Opposable thumbs on hind feet.

Rabbit

REAR

FRONT

Larger hind feet, smaller front feet. Hoppers producing a "Y" shaped track.

Skunk

FRONT

REAR

Five toes on their hind and front feet. Front and rear are approximately same size. Claws show up in many prints.

Otter

FRONT   REAR

Five toes and short claws give their prints a pointed look. Toes are partially webbed.

Armadillo

REAR

FRONT

Four long toe prints with sharp claw at tip. Front print show distinct "V" between middle toes.

Sketch

_____
_____
_____
_____
_____
_____
_____
_____
_____
_____
_____
_____

General

Date: _____ Location: _____

Environment: ◯ Mud ◯ Snow ◯ Soft Garden Soil ◯ Sand

Time of Day: ◯ Morning ◯ Midday ◯ Evening ◯ Time _____

Front Toes: ◯ Five ◯ Four ◯ Three ◯ Two

Rear Toes: ◯ Five ◯ Four ◯ Three ◯ Two

Track Symmetry: ◯ Symmetric ◯ Asymmetric

Claws / Nails: ◯ Visible ◯ Not Visible   Webbing: ◯ Yes ◯ No

Surroundings: _____

Movement Pattern: ◯ Zig-Zaggler ◯ Trot ◯ Lope ◯ Gallop

Notes: _____

Canine

Wolf

FRONT   REAR

Biggest in this group with a long (4") and wide print.

Coyote
FRONT   REAR

Slightly smaller than wolves with print more narrow (2.5 to 3.5").

Fox
FRONT   REAR

Smallest in the group with print (2 to 3") and fuzzy around edges.

Dog
FRONT   REAR

Similar to wolf/coyote with thicker nails.

Feline

Cougar / Mountain Lion
FRONT   REAR

Largest in the group (greater than 3"). Size of domestic dog.

Lynx
FRONT   REAR

Same as cougar but smaller in size and not as defined due to fur around paws.

Bobcat
FRONT   REAR

Smaller tracks (2"). Often confused with coyote or fox but lacks nails. Round shape.

House Cat
FRONT   REAR

Small (1 to 1.5"). Similar to domestic dog, meander when walking.

Bird

Crow
Standard bird track: 3 forward, 1 rear. Print 2-2.5".

Grouse
Small ground birds with only 3 forward toes. Print 2" long.

Turkey
Similar to grouse but much larger prints (4") long.

Duck
Webbing gives its print distinctive shape.

Bear

Black Bear
FRONT   REAR

Has short claws and its toes spread out in a curve over its foot pad. Generally going to be smaller than grizzly bear paw.

Grizzly Bear
FRONT   REAR

Has long claws that extend out further from their toes. Its toes also are held closer together, forming almost a straight line above the foot pad.

Rodent

Beaver

FRONT   REAR
Webbed hind feet with 5 toes (4.5-7"). Sometime 4-toed prints.

Porcupine
FRONT   REAR
Usually only see pads in prints (1-2"). Pigeon-toed.

Muskrat
FRONT   REAR
Hand-like like raccoon but smaller (2.3").

Mouse

FRONT   REAR
Larger back feet (1.5 - 2"), smaller front feet (0.25-0.5").

Squirrel

FRONT   REAR
Larger back feet (1.5-2"), smaller front feet (1-1.5").

Hoof

Mountain Goat

FRONT   REAR
Have toes that spread when they step, creating a distinctive V shape at the top of their print.

Bighorn Sheep

FRONT   REAR
Similar to deer but with straighter edges and less pointed. More blocky and less shaped like a heart.

Wild Hog

FRONT   REAR
Often confused with deer but toes are wider, rounder and blunter and don't come to a point. Have dew claw that rests slightly outside print.

Reptile / Amphibian

Alligator

FRONT
REAR
Large feet with four toes on front prints and five toes on rear prints. Front are wide in heel, rear are longer, narrow and pointed heel.

Lizard

FRONT   REAR
Lightweight and don't leave much of a track. Might leave small scuff from feet and small tail drag.

Frog

FRONT   REAR
Have four bulbous toes in front and five in hind prints. Front toes point slightly inward producing a "K" shaped print, while rear toes slope upward and outward.

Other Common

Raccoon

FRONT
REAR
Five toes resembles hand of a baby. Front print smaller (1-3") with C-shaped heel pad. Rear print longer (1.5-4") heel pad.

Opossum

FRONT   REAR
Five fingers and human hand shape. Opposable thumbs on hind feet.

Rabbit
REAR

FRONT
Larger hind feet, smaller front feet. Hoppers producing a "Y" shaped track.

Skunk

FRONT
REAR
Five toes on their hind and front feet. Front and rear are approximately same size. Claws show up in many prints.

Otter

FRONT   REAR
Five toes and short claws give their prints a pointed look. Toes are partially webbed.

Armadillo

REAR
FRONT
Four long toe prints with sharp claw at tip. Front print show distinct "V" between middle toes.

Sketch / Notes

Sketch

_____
_____
_____
_____
_____
_____
_____
_____
_____
_____
_____

General

Date: _____ Location: _____

Environment: ○ Mud ○ Snow ○ Soft Garden Soil ○ Sand

Time of Day: ○ Morning ○ Midday ○ Evening ○ Time _____

Front Toes: ○ Five ○ Four ○ Three ○ Two

Rear Toes: ○ Five ○ Four ○ Three ○ Two

Track Symmetry: ○ Symmetric ○ Asymmetric

Claws / Nails: ○ Visible ○ Not Visible   Webbing: ○ Yes ○ No

Surroundings: _____

Movement Pattern: ○ Zig-Zaggler ○ Trot ○ Lope ○ Gallop

Notes: _____

Canine

Wolf
FRONT   REAR
Biggest in this group with a long (4") and wide print.

Coyote
FRONT   REAR
Slightly smaller than wolves with print more narrow (2.5 to 3.5").

Fox
FRONT   REAR
Smallest in the group with print (2 to 3") and fuzzy around edges.

Dog
FRONT   REAR
Similar to wolf/coyote with thicker nails.

Feline

Cougar / Mountain Lion
FRONT   REAR
Largest in the group (greater than 3"). Size of domestic dog.

Lynx
FRONT   REAR
Same as cougar but smaller in size and not as defined due to fur around paws.

Bobcat
FRONT   REAR
Smaller tracks (2"). Often confused with coyote or fox but lacks nails. Round shape.

House Cat
FRONT   REAR
Small (1 to 1.5"). Similar to domestic dog, meander when walking.

Bird

Crow
Standard bird track: 3 forward, 1 rear. Print 2-2.5".

Grouse
Small ground birds with only 3 forward toes. Print 2" long.

Turkey
Similar to grouse but much larger prints (4") long.

Duck
Webbing gives its print distinctive shape.

Bear

Black Bear

FRONT   REAR
Has short claws and its toes spread out in a curve over its foot pad Generally going to be smaller than grizzly bear paw.

Grizzly Bear

FRONT   REAR
Has long claws that extend out further from their toes. Its toes also are held closer together, forming almost a straight line above the foot pad.

Rodent

Beaver

FRONT   REAR
Webbed hind feet with 5 toes (4.5-7"). Sometime 4-toed prints.

Porcupine

FRONT   REAR
Usually only see pads in prints (1-2"). Pigeon-toed.

Muskrat

FRONT   REAR
Hand-like like raccoon but smaller (2.3").

Mouse

FRONT   REAR
Larger back feet (1.5 - 2"), smaller front feet (0.25-0.5").

Squirrel
FRONT   REAR
Larger back feet (1.5-2"), smaller front feet (1-1.5").

Hoof

Mountain Goat

FRONT   REAR
Have toes that spread when they step, creating a distinctive V shape at the top of their print.

Bighorn Sheep

FRONT   REAR
Similar to deer but with straighter edges and less pointed. More blocky and less shaped like a heart.

Wild Hog

FRONT   REAR
Often confused with deer but toes are wider, rounder and blunter and don't come to a point. Have dew claw that rests slightly outside print.

Reptile / Amphibian

Alligator

FRONT
REAR
Large feet with four toes on front prints and five toes on rear prints. Front are wide in heel, rear are longer, narrow and pointed heel.

Lizard

FRONT   REAR
Lightweight and don't leave much of a track. Might leave small scuff from feet and small tail drag.

Frog

FRONT   REAR
Have four bulbous toes in front and five in hind prints. Front toes point slightly inward producing a "K" shaped print, while rear toes slope upward and outward.

Other Common

Raccoon

FRONT
REAR
Five toes resembles hand of a baby. Front print smaller (1-3") with C-shaped heel pad. Rear print longer (1.5-4") heel pad.

Opossum

FRONT   REAR
Five fingers and human hand shape. Opposable thumbs on hind feet.

Rabbit
REAR

FRONT
Larger hind feet, smaller front feet. Hoppers producing a "Y" shaped track.

Skunk

FRONT   REAR
Five toes on their hind and front feet. Front and rear are approximately same size. Claws show up in many prints.

Otter

FRONT   REAR
Five toes and short claws give their prints a pointed look. Toes are partially webbed.

Armadillo
REAR

FRONT
Four long toe prints with sharp claw at tip. Front print show distinct "V" between middle toes.

Sketch / Notes

Sketch

_____
_____
_____
_____
_____
_____
_____
_____
_____
_____
_____

General

Date: _____ Location: _____

Environment: ○ Mud ○ Snow ○ Soft Garden Soil ○ Sand

Time of Day: ○ Morning ○ Midday ○ Evening ○ Time _____

Front Toes: ○ Five ○ Four ○ Three ○ Two

Rear Toes: ○ Five ○ Four ○ Three ○ Two

Track Symmetry: ○ Symmetric ○ Asymmetric

Claws / Nails: ○ Visible ○ Not Visible   Webbing: ○ Yes ○ No

Surroundings: _____

Movement Pattern: ○ Zig-Zaggler ○ Trot ○ Lope ○ Gallop

Notes: _____

Canine

Wolf

FRONT   REAR

Biggest in this group with a long (4") and wide print.

Coyote
FRONT   REAR

Slightly smaller than wolves with print more narrow (2.5 to 3.5").

Fox
FRONT   REAR

Smallest in the group with print (2 to 3") and fuzzy around edges.

Dog
FRONT   REAR

Similar to wolf/coyote with thicker nails.

Feline

Cougar / Mountain Lion
FRONT   REAR

Largest in the group (greater than 3"). Size of domestic dog.

Lynx

FRONT   REAR

Same as cougar but smaller in size and not as defined due to fur around paws.

Bobcat

FRONT   REAR

Smaller tracks (2"). Often confused with coyote or fox but lacks nails. Round shape.

House Cat

FRONT   REAR

Small (1 to 1.5"). Similar to domestic dog, meander when walking.

Bird

Crow

Standard bird track: 3 forward, 1 rear. Print 2-2.5".

Grouse

Small ground birds with only 3 forward toes. Print 2" long.

Turkey

Similar to grouse but much larger prints (4") long.

Duck

Webbing gives its print distinctive shape.

Bear

Black Bear

FRONT   REAR

Has short claws and its toes spread out in a curve over its foot pad. Generally going to be smaller than grizzly bear paw.

Grizzly Bear

FRONT   REAR

Has long claws that extend out further from their toes. Its toes also are held closer together, forming almost a straight line above the foot pad.

Rodent

Beaver

FRONT REAR
Webbed hind feet with 5 toes (4.5-7"). Sometime 4-toed prints.

Porcupine

FRONT REAR
Usually only see pads in prints (1-2"). Pigeon-toed.

Muskrat

FRONT REAR
Hand-like like raccoon but smaller (2.3").

Mouse

FRONT REAR
Larger back feet (1.5 - 2"), smaller front feet (0.25-0.5").

Squirrel

FRONT REAR
Larger back feet (1.5-2"), smaller front feet (1-1.5").

Hoof

Mountain Goat

FRONT REAR
Have toes that spread when they step, creating a distinctive V shape at the top of their print.

Bighorn Sheep

FRONT REAR
Similar to deer but with straighter edges and less pointed. More blocky and less shaped like a heart.

Wild Hog

FRONT REAR
Often confused with deer but toes are wider, rounder and blunter and don't come to a point. Have dew claw that rests slightly outside print.

Reptile / Amphibian

Alligator

FRONT
REAR
Large feet with four toes on front prints and five toes on rear prints. Front are wide in heel, rear are longer, narrow and pointed heel.

Lizard

FRONT REAR
Lightweight and don't leave much of a track. Might leave small scuff from feet and small tail drag.

Frog

FRONT REAR
Have four bulbous toes in front and five in hind prints. Front toes point slightly inward producing a "K" shaped print, while rear toes slope upward and outward.

Other Common

Raccoon

FRONT
REAR
Five toes resembles hand of a baby. Front print smaller (1-3") with C-shaped heel pad. Rear print longer (1.5-4") heel pad.

Opossum

FRONT REAR
Five fingers and human hand shape. Opposable thumbs on hind feet .

Rabbit

REAR
FRONT
Larger hind feet, smaller front feet. Hoppers producing a "Y" shaped track.

Skunk

FRONT
REAR
Five toes on their hind and front feet. Front and rear are approximately same size. Claws show up in many prints.

Otter

FRONT REAR
Five toes and short claws give their prints a pointed look. Toes are partially webbed.

Armadillo
REAR
FRONT
Four long toe prints with sharp claw at tip. Front print show distinct "V" between middle toes.

Sketch / Notes

Sketch

_____
_____
_____
_____
_____
_____
_____
_____
_____
_____
_____
_____

General

Date: _____ Location: _____

Environment: ◯ Mud ◯ Snow ◯ Soft Garden Soil ◯ Sand

Time of Day: ◯ Morning ◯ Midday ◯ Evening ◯ Time_____

Front Toes: ◯ Five ◯ Four ◯ Three ◯ Two

Rear Toes: ◯ Five ◯ Four ◯ Three ◯ Two

Track Symmetry: ◯ Symmetric ◯ Asymmetric

Claws / Nails: ◯ Visible ◯ Not Visible   Webbing: ◯ Yes ◯ No

Surroundings: _____

Movement Pattern: ◯ Zig-Zaggler ◯ Trot ◯ Lope ◯ Gallop

Notes: _____

Canine

Wolf

FRONT   REAR

Biggest in this group with a long (4") and wide print.

Coyote

FRONT   REAR

Slightly smaller than wolves with print more narrow (2.5 to 3.5").

Fox

FRONT   REAR

Smallest in the group with print (2 to 3") and fuzzy around edges.

Dog

FRONT   REAR

Similar to wolf/coyote with thicker nails.

Feline

Cougar / Mountain Lion

FRONT   REAR

Largest in the group (greater than 3"). Size of domestic dog.

Lynx

FRONT   REAR

Same as cougar but smaller in size and not as defined due to fur around paws.

Bobcat

FRONT   REAR

Smaller tracks (2"). Often confused with coyote or fox but lacks nails. Round shape.

House Cat

FRONT   REAR

Small (1 to 1.5"). Similar to domestic dog, meander when walking.

Bird

Crow

Standard bird track: 3 forward, 1 rear. Print 2-2.5".

Grouse

Small ground birds with only 3 forward toes. Print 2" long.

Turkey

Similar to grouse but much larger prints (4") long.

Duck

Webbing gives its print distinctive shape.

Bear

Black Bear
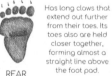
FRONT   REAR

Has short claws and its toes spread out in a curve over its foot pad. Generally going to be smaller than grizzly bear paw.

Grizzly Bear
FRONT   REAR

Has long claws that extend out further from their toes. Its toes also are held closer together, forming almost a straight line above the foot pad.

Rodent

Beaver

FRONT REAR
Webbed hind feet with 5 toes (4.5-7"). Sometime 4-toed prints.

Porcupine

FRONT REAR
Usually only see pads in prints (1-2"). Pigeon-toed.

Muskrat

FRONT REAR
Hand-like like raccoon but smaller (2.3").

Mouse

FRONT REAR
Larger back feet (1.5 - 2"), smaller front feet (0.25-0.5").

Squirrel
FRONT REAR
Larger back feet (1.5-2"), smaller front feet (1-1.5").

Hoof

Mountain Goat

FRONT REAR
Have toes that spread when they step, creating a distinctive V shape at the top of their print.

Bighorn Sheep

FRONT REAR
Similar to deer but with straighter edges and less pointed. More blocky and less shaped like a heart.

Wild Hog

FRONT REAR
Often confused with deer but toes are wider, rounder and blunter and don't come to a point. Have dew claw that rests slightly outside print.

Reptile / Amphibian

Alligator

FRONT
REAR
Large feet with four toes on front prints and five toes on rear prints. Front are wide in heel, rear are longer, narrow and pointed heel.

Lizard

FRONT REAR
Lightweight and don't leave much of a track. Might leave small scuff from feet and small tail drag.

Frog

FRONT REAR
Have four bulbous toes in front and five in hind prints. Front toes point slightly inward producing a "K" shaped print, while rear toes slope upward and outward.

Other Common

Raccoon

FRONT
REAR
Five toes resembles hand of a baby. Front print smaller (1-3") with C-shaped heel pad. Rear print longer (1.5-4") heel pad.

Opossum

FRONT REAR
Five fingers and human hand shape. Opposable thumbs on hind feet.

Rabbit
REAR

FRONT
Larger hind feet, smaller front feet. Hoppers producing a "Y" shaped track.

Skunk

FRONT
REAR
Five toes on their hind and front feet. Front and rear are approximately same size. Claws show up in many prints.

Otter

FRONT REAR
Five toes and short claws give their prints a pointed look. Toes are partially webbed.

Armadillo
REAR

FRONT
Four long toe prints with sharp claw at tip. Front print show distinct "V" between middle toes.

Sketch / Notes

Sketch

_____
_____
_____
_____
_____
_____
_____
_____
_____
_____
_____

General

Date: _____ Location: _____

Environment: ◯ Mud ◯ Snow ◯ Soft Garden Soil ◯ Sand

Time of Day: ◯ Morning ◯ Midday ◯ Evening ◯ Time _____

Front Toes: ◯ Five ◯ Four ◯ Three ◯ Two

Rear Toes: ◯ Five ◯ Four ◯ Three ◯ Two

Track Symmetry: ◯ Symmetric ◯ Asymmetric

Claws / Nails: ◯ Visible ◯ Not Visible   Webbing: ◯ Yes ◯ No

Surroundings: _____

Movement Pattern: ◯ Zig-Zaggler ◯ Trot ◯ Lope ◯ Gallop

Notes: _____

Canine

Wolf	Coyote	Fox	Dog
FRONT REAR	FRONT REAR	FRONT REAR	FRONT REAR
Biggest in this group with a long (4") and wide print.	Slightly smaller than wolves with print more narrow (2.5 to 3.5").	Smallest in the group with print (2 to 3") and fuzzy around edges.	Similar to wolf/coyote with thicker nails.

Feline

Cougar / Mountain Lion	Lynx	Bobcat	House Cat
FRONT REAR	FRONT REAR	FRONT REAR	FRONT REAR
Largest in the group (greater than 3"). Size of domestic dog.	Same as cougar but smaller in size and not as defined due to fur around paws.	Smaller tracks (2"). Often confused with coyote or fox but lacks nails. Round shape.	Small (1 to 1.5"). Similar to domestic dog, meander when walking.

Bird

Crow	Grouse	Turkey	Duck
Standard bird track: 3 forward, 1 rear. Print 2-2.5".	Small ground birds with only 3 forward toes. Print 2" long.	Similar to grouse but much larger prints (4") long.	Webbing gives its print distinctive shape.

Bear

Black Bear

FRONT REAR

Has short claws and its toes spread out in a curve over its foot pad Generally going to be smaller than grizzly bear paw.

Grizzly Bear

FRONT REAR

Has long claws that extend out further from their toes. Its toes also are held closer together, forming almost a straight line above the foot pad.

Rodent

Beaver

FRONT   REAR
Webbed hind feet with 5 toes (4.5-7"). Sometime 4-toed prints.

Porcupine

FRONT REAR
Usually only see pads in prints (1-2"). Pigeon-toed.

Muskrat

FRONT   REAR
Hand-like like raccoon but smaller (2.3").

Mouse

FRONT   REAR
Larger back feet (1.5 - 2"), smaller front feet (0.25-0.5").

Squirrel

FRONT   REAR
Larger back feet (1.5-2"), smaller front feet (1-1.5").

Hoof

Mountain Goat

FRONT   REAR
Have toes that spread when they step, creating a distinctive V shape at the top of their print.

Bighorn Sheep

FRONT   REAR
Similar to deer but with straighter edges and less pointed. More blocky and less shaped like a heart.

Wild Hog

FRONT   REAR
Often confused with deer but toes are wider, rounder and blunter and don't come to a point. Have dew claw that rests slightly outside print.

Reptile / Amphibian

Alligator

FRONT
REAR
Large feet with four toes on front prints and five toes on rear prints. Front are wide in heel, rear are longer, narrow and pointed heel.

Lizard

FRONT   REAR
Lightweight and don't leave much of a track. Might leave small scuff from feet and small tail drag.

Frog

FRONT   REAR
Have four bulbous toes in front and five in hind prints. Front toes point slightly inward producing a "K" shaped print, while rear toes slope upward and outward.

Other Common

Raccoon

FRONT
REAR
Five toes resembles hand of a baby. Front print smaller (1-3") with C-shaped heel pad. Rear print longer (1.5-4") heel pad.

Opossum

FRONT   REAR
Five fingers and human hand shape. Opposable thumbs on hind feet .

Rabbit
REAR

FRONT
Larger hind feet, smaller front feet. Hoppers producing a "Y" shaped track.

Skunk

FRONT
REAR
Five toes on their hind and front feet. Front and rear are approximately same size. Claws show up in many prints.

Otter

FRONT   REAR
Five toes and short claws give their prints a pointed look. Toes are partially webbed.

Armadillo
REAR

FRONT
Four long toe prints with sharp claw at tip. Front print show distinct "V" between middle toes.

Sketch / Notes

Sketch

_____
_____
_____
_____
_____
_____
_____
_____
_____
_____
_____

General

Date: _____ Location: _____

Environment: ◯ Mud ◯ Snow ◯ Soft Garden Soil ◯ Sand

Time of Day: ◯ Morning ◯ Midday ◯ Evening ◯ Time _____

Front Toes: ◯ Five ◯ Four ◯ Three ◯ Two

Rear Toes: ◯ Five ◯ Four ◯ Three ◯ Two

Track Symmetry: ◯ Symmetric ◯ Asymmetric

Claws / Nails: ◯ Visible ◯ Not Visible   Webbing: ◯ Yes ◯ No

Surroundings: _____

Movement Pattern: ◯ Zig-Zaggler ◯ Trot ◯ Lope ◯ Gallop

Notes: _____

Canine

Wolf

FRONT REAR

Biggest in this group with a long (4") and wide print.

Coyote
FRONT REAR

Slightly smaller than wolves with print more narrow (2.5 to 3.5").

Fox
FRONT REAR

Smallest in the group with print (2 to 3") and fuzzy around edges.

Dog
FRONT REAR

Similar to wolf/coyote with thicker nails.

Feline

Cougar / Mountain Lion

FRONT REAR

Largest in the group (greater than 3"). Size of domestic dog.

Lynx

FRONT REAR

Same as cougar but smaller in size and not as defined due to fur around paws.

Bobcat
FRONT REAR

Smaller tracks (2"). Often confused with coyote or fox but lacks nails. Round shape.

House Cat
FRONT REAR

Small (1 to 1.5"). Similar to domestic dog, meander when walking.

Bird

Crow

Standard bird track: 3 forward, 1 rear. Print 2-2.5".

Grouse

Small ground birds with only 3 forward toes. Print 2" long.

Turkey

Similar to grouse but much larger prints (4") long.

Duck

Webbing gives its print distinctive shape.

Bear

Black Bear

FRONT REAR

Has short claws and its toes spread out in a curve over its foot pad. Generally going to be smaller than grizzly bear paw.

Grizzly Bear

FRONT REAR

Has long claws that extend out further from their toes. Its toes also are held closer together, forming almost a straight line above the foot pad.

Beaver

FRONT REAR

Webbed hind feet with 5 toes (4.5-7"). Sometime 4-toed prints.

Porcupine

FRONT REAR

Usually only see pads in prints (1-2"). Pigeon-toed.

Muskrat

FRONT REAR

Hand-like like raccoon but smaller (2.3").

Mouse

FRONT REAR

Larger back feet (1.5 - 2"), smaller front feet (0.25-0.5").

Squirrel

FRONT REAR

Larger back feet (1.5-2"), smaller front feet (1-1.5").

Mountain Goat

FRONT REAR

Have toes that spread when they step, creating a distinctive V shape at the top of their print.

Bighorn Sheep

FRONT REAR

Similar to deer but with straighter edges and less pointed. More blocky and less shaped like a heart.

Wild Hog

FRONT REAR

Often confused with deer but toes are wider, rounder and blunter and don't come to a point. Have dew claw that rests slightly outside print.

Alligator

FRONT

REAR

Large feet with four toes on front prints and five toes on rear prints. Front are wide in heel, rear are longer, narrow and pointed heel.

Lizard

FRONT REAR

Lightweight and don't leave much of a track. Might leave small scuff from feet and small tail drag.

Frog

FRONT REAR

Have four bulbous toes in front and five in hind prints. Front toes point slightly inward producing a "K" shaped print, while rear toes slope upward and outward.

Raccoon

FRONT

REAR

Five toes resembles hand of a baby. Front print smaller (1-3") with C-shaped heel pad. Rear print longer (1.5-4") heel pad.

Opossum

FRONT REAR

Five fingers and human hand shape. Opposable thumbs on hind feet .

Rabbit

REAR

FRONT

Larger hind feet, smaller front feet. Hoppers producing a "Y" shaped track.

Skunk

FRONT

REAR

Five toes on their hind and front feet. Front and rear are approximately same size. Claws show up in many prints.

Otter

FRONT REAR

Five toes and short claws give their prints a pointed look. Toes are partially webbed.

Armadillo

REAR

FRONT

Four long toe prints with sharp claw at tip. Front print show distinct "V" between middle toes.

Sketch

_____
_____
_____
_____
_____
_____
_____
_____
_____
_____
_____
_____

General

Date: _____ Location: _____

Environment: ◯ Mud ◯ Snow ◯ Soft Garden Soil ◯ Sand

Time of Day: ◯ Morning ◯ Midday ◯ Evening ◯ Time _____

Front Toes: ◯ Five ◯ Four ◯ Three ◯ Two

Rear Toes: ◯ Five ◯ Four ◯ Three ◯ Two

Track Symmetry: ◯ Symmetric ◯ Asymmetric

Claws / Nails: ◯ Visible ◯ Not Visible   Webbing: ◯ Yes ◯ No

Surroundings: _____

Movement Pattern: ◯ Zig-Zaggler ◯ Trot ◯ Lope ◯ Gallop

Notes: _____

Canine

Wolf

FRONT   REAR

Biggest in this group with a long (4") and wide print.

Coyote

FRONT   REAR

Slightly smaller than wolves with print more narrow (2.5 to 3.5").

Fox

FRONT   REAR

Smallest in the group with print (2 to 3") and fuzzy around edges.

Dog

FRONT   REAR

Similar to wolf/coyote with thicker nails.

Feline

Cougar / Mountain Lion

FRONT   REAR

Largest in the group (greater than 3"). Size of domestic dog.

Lynx

FRONT   REAR

Same as cougar but smaller in size and not as defined due to fur around paws.

Bobcat

FRONT   REAR

Smaller tracks (2"). Often confused with coyote or fox but lacks nails. Round shape.

House Cat

FRONT   REAR

Small (1 to 1.5"). Similar to domestic dog, meander when walking.

Bird

Crow

Standard bird track: 3 forward, 1 rear. Print 2-2.5".

Grouse

Small ground birds with only 3 forward toes. Print 2" long.

Turkey

Similar to grouse but much larger prints (4") long.

Duck

Webbing gives its print distinctive shape.

Bear

Black Bear

FRONT   REAR

Has short claws and its toes spread out in a curve over its foot pad. Generally going to be smaller than grizzly bear paw.

Grizzly Bear

FRONT   REAR

Has long claws that extend out further from their toes. Its toes also are held closer together, forming almost a straight line above the foot pad.

Rodent

Beaver	Porcupine	Muskrat	Mouse	Squirrel

FRONT REAR | FRONT REAR | FRONT REAR | FRONT REAR | FRONT REAR

Webbed hind feet with 5 toes (4.5-7). Sometime 4-toed prints.

Usually only see pads in prints (1-2). Pigeon-toed.

Hand-like like raccoon but smaller (2.3").

Larger back feet (1.5 - 2"), smaller front feet (0.25-0.5").

Larger back feet (1.5-2"), smaller front feet (1-1.5").

Hoof

Mountain Goat

FRONT REAR

Have toes that spread when they step, creating a distinctive V shape at the top of their print.

Bighorn Sheep

FRONT REAR

Similar to deer but with straighter edges and less pointed. More blocky and less shaped like a heart.

Wild Hog

FRONT REAR

Often confused with deer but toes are wider, rounder and blunter and don't come to a point. Have dew claw that rests slightly outside print.

Reptile / Amphibian

Alligator

FRONT

REAR

Large feet with four toes on front prints and five toes on rear prints. Front are wide in heel, rear are longer, narrow and pointed heel.

Lizard

FRONT REAR

Lightweight and don't leave much of a track. Might leave small scuff from feet and small tail drag.

Frog

FRONT REAR

Have four bulbous toes in front and five in hind prints. Front toes point slightly inward producing a "K" shaped print, while rear toes slope upward and outward.

Other Common

Raccoon

FRONT

REAR

Five toes resembles hand of a baby. Front print smaller (1-3") with C-shaped heel pad. Rear print longer (1.5-4") heel pad.

Opossum

FRONT REAR

Five fingers and human hand shape. Opposable thumbs on hind feet .

Rabbit

REAR

FRONT

Larger hind feet, smaller front feet. Hoppers producing a "Y" shaped track.

Skunk

FRONT

REAR

Five toes on their hind and front feet. Front and rear are approximately same size. Claws show up in many prints.

Otter

FRONT REAR

Five toes and short claws give their prints a pointed look. Toes are partially webbed.

Armadillo

REAR

FRONT

Four long toe prints with sharp claw at tip. Front print show distinct "V" between middle toes.

Sketch / Notes

Sketch

_____
_____
_____
_____
_____
_____
_____
_____
_____
_____
_____
_____

General

Date: _____   Location: _____

Environment: ◯ Mud   ◯ Snow   ◯ Soft Garden Soil   ◯ Sand

Time of Day: ◯ Morning   ◯ Midday   ◯ Evening   ◯ Time _____

Front Toes: ◯ Five   ◯ Four   ◯ Three   ◯ Two

Rear Toes: ◯ Five   ◯ Four   ◯ Three   ◯ Two

Track Symmetry: ◯ Symmetric   ◯ Asymmetric

Claws / Nails: ◯ Visible   ◯ Not Visible   Webbing: ◯ Yes   ◯ No

Surroundings: _____

Movement Pattern: ◯ Zig-Zaggler   ◯ Trot   ◯ Lope   ◯ Gallop

Notes: _____

Canine

Wolf

FRONT   REAR

Biggest in this group with a long (4") and wide print.

Coyote
FRONT   REAR

Slightly smaller than wolves with print more narrow (2.5 to 3.5").

Fox
FRONT   REAR

Smallest in the group with print (2 to 3") and fuzzy around edges.

Dog
FRONT   REAR

Similar to wolf/coyote with thicker nails.

Feline

Cougar / Mountain Lion

FRONT   REAR

Largest in the group (greater than 3"). Size of domestic dog.

Lynx

FRONT   REAR

Same as cougar but smaller in size and not as defined due to fur around paws.

Bobcat

FRONT   REAR

Smaller tracks (2"). Often confused with coyote or fox but lacks nails. Round shape.

House Cat

FRONT   REAR

Small (1 to 1.5"). Similar to domestic dog, meander when walking.

Bird

Crow
FRONT

Standard bird track: 3 forward, 1 rear. Print 2-2.5".

Grouse

Small ground birds with only 3 forward toes. Print 2" long.

Turkey

Similar to grouse but much larger prints (4") long.

Duck

Webbing gives its print distinctive shape.

Bear

Black Bear

FRONT   REAR

Has short claws and its toes spread out in a curve over its foot pad. Generally going to be smaller than grizzly bear paw.

Grizzly Bear

FRONT   REAR

Has long claws that extend out further from their toes. Its toes also are held closer together, forming almost a straight line above the foot pad.

Beaver

FRONT   REAR

Webbed hind feet with 5 toes (4.5-7"). Sometime 4-toed prints.

Porcupine

FRONT   REAR

Usually only see pads in prints (1-2"). Pigeon-toed.

Muskrat

FRONT   REAR

Hand-like like raccoon but smaller (2.3").

Mouse

FRONT   REAR

Larger back feet (1.5 - 2"), smaller front feet (0.25-0.5").

Squirrel

FRONT   REAR

Larger back feet (1.5-2"), smaller front feet (1-1.5").

Mountain Goat

FRONT   REAR

Have toes that spread when they step, creating a distinctive V shape at the top of their print.

Bighorn Sheep

FRONT   REAR

Similar to deer but with straighter edges and less pointed. More blocky and less shaped like a heart.

Wild Hog

FRONT   REAR

Often confused with deer but toes are wider, rounder and blunter and don't come to a point. Have dew claw that rests slightly outside print.

Alligator

FRONT

REAR

Large feet with four toes on front prints and five toes on rear prints. Front are wide in heel, rear are longer, narrow and pointed heel.

Lizard

FRONT   REAR

Lightweight and don't leave much of a track. Might leave small scuff from feet and small tail drag.

Frog

FRONT   REAR

Have four bulbous toes in front and five in hind prints. Front toes point slightly inward producing a "K" shaped print, while rear toes slope upward and outward.

Raccoon

FRONT

REAR

Five toes resembles hand of a baby. Front print smaller (1-3") with C-shaped heel pad. Rear print longer (1.5-4") heel pad.

Opossum

FRONT   REAR

Five fingers and human hand shape. Opposable thumbs on hind feet.

Rabbit

REAR

FRONT

Larger hind feet, smaller front feet. Hoppers producing a "Y" shaped track.

Skunk

FRONT

REAR

Five toes on their hind and front feet. Front and rear are approximately same size. Claws show up in many prints.

Otter

FRONT   REAR

Five toes and short claws give their prints a pointed look. Toes are partially webbed.

Armadillo

REAR

FRONT

Four long toe prints with sharp claw at tip. Front print show distinct "V" between middle toes.

Sketch

_____
_____
_____
_____
_____
_____
_____
_____
_____
_____
_____

General

Date: _____ Location: _____

Environment: ⬭ Mud ⬭ Snow ⬭ Soft Garden Soil ⬭ Sand

Time of Day: ⬭ Morning ⬭ Midday ⬭ Evening ⬭ Time _____

Front Toes: ⬭ Five ⬭ Four ⬭ Three ⬭ Two

Rear Toes: ⬭ Five ⬭ Four ⬭ Three ⬭ Two

Track Symmetry: ⬭ Symmetric ⬭ Asymmetric

Claws / Nails: ⬭ Visible ⬭ Not Visible   Webbing: ⬭ Yes ⬭ No

Surroundings: _____

Movement Pattern: ⬭ Zig-Zaggler ⬭ Trot ⬭ Lope ⬭ Gallop

Notes: _____

Canine

Wolf
FRONT REAR

Biggest in this group with a long (4") and wide print.

Coyote
FRONT REAR

Slightly smaller than wolves with print more narrow (2.5 to 3.5").

Fox
FRONT REAR

Smallest in the group with print (2 to 3") and fuzzy around edges.

Dog
FRONT REAR

Similar to wolf/coyote with thicker nails.

Feline

Cougar / Mountain Lion
FRONT REAR

Largest in the group (greater than 3"). Size of domestic dog.

Lynx
FRONT REAR

Same as cougar but smaller in size and not as defined due to fur around paws.

Bobcat
FRONT REAR

Smaller tracks (2"). Often confused with coyote or fox but lacks nails. Round shape.

House Cat
FRONT REAR

Small (1 to 1.5"). Similar to domestic dog, meander when walking.

Bird

Crow

Standard bird track: 3 forward, 1 rear. Print 2-2.5".

Grouse

Small ground birds with only 3 forward toes. Print 2" long.

Turkey

Similar to grouse but much larger prints (4") long.

Duck

Webbing gives its print distinctive shape.

Bear

Black Bear
FRONT REAR

Has short claws and its toes spread out in a curve over its foot pad. Generally going to be smaller than grizzly bear paw.

Grizzly Bear
FRONT REAR

Has long claws that extend out further from their toes. Its toes also are held closer together, forming almost a straight line above the foot pad.

Beaver

FRONT   REAR

Webbed hind feet with 5 toes (4.5-7"). Sometime 4-toed prints.

Porcupine

FRONT   REAR

Usually only see pads in prints (1-2"). Pigeon-toed.

Muskrat

FRONT   REAR

Hand-like like raccoon but smaller (2.3").

Mouse

FRONT   REAR

Larger back feet (1.5 - 2), smaller front feet (0.25-0.5").

Squirrel

FRONT   REAR

Larger back feet (1.5-2"), smaller front feet (1-1.5").

Mountain Goat

FRONT   REAR

Have toes that spread when they step, creating a distinctive V shape at the top of their print.

Bighorn Sheep

FRONT   REAR

Similar to deer but with straighter edges and less pointed. More blocky and less shaped like a heart.

Wild Hog

FRONT   REAR

Often confused with deer but toes are wider, rounder and blunter and don't come to a point. Have dew claw that rests slightly outside print.

Alligator

FRONT

REAR

Large feet with four toes on front prints and five toes on rear prints. Front are wide in heel, rear are longer, narrow and pointed heel.

Lizard

FRONT   REAR

Lightweight and don't leave much of a track. Might leave small scuff from feet and small tail drag.

Frog

FRONT   REAR

Have four bulbous toes in front and five in hind prints. Front toes point slightly inward producing a "K" shaped print, while rear toes slope upward and outward.

Raccoon

FRONT

REAR

Five toes resembles hand of a baby. Front print smaller (1-3") with C-shaped heel pad. Rear print longer (1.5-4") heel pad.

Opossum

FRONT   REAR

Five fingers and human hand shape. Opposable thumbs on hind feet .

Rabbit

REAR

FRONT

Larger hind feet, smaller front feet. Hoppers producing a "Y" shaped track.

Skunk

FRONT   REAR

Five toes on their hind and front feet. Front and rear are approximately same size. Claws show up in many prints.

Otter

FRONT   REAR

Five toes and short claws give their prints a pointed look. Toes are partially webbed.

Armadillo

REAR

FRONT

Four long toe prints with sharp claw at tip. Front print show distinct "V" between middle toes.

Sketch

_____
_____
_____
_____
_____
_____
_____
_____
_____
_____
_____
_____

General

Date: _____ Location: _____

Environment: ◯ Mud ◯ Snow ◯ Soft Garden Soil ◯ Sand

Time of Day: ◯ Morning ◯ Midday ◯ Evening ◯ Time _____

Front Toes: ◯ Five ◯ Four ◯ Three ◯ Two

Rear Toes: ◯ Five ◯ Four ◯ Three ◯ Two

Track Symmetry: ◯ Symmetric ◯ Asymmetric

Claws / Nails: ◯ Visible ◯ Not Visible   Webbing: ◯ Yes ◯ No

Surroundings: _____

Movement Pattern: ◯ Zig-Zaggler ◯ Trot ◯ Lope ◯ Gallop

Notes: _____

Canine

Wolf

FRONT   REAR

Biggest in this group with a long (4") and wide print.

Coyote
FRONT   REAR

Slightly smaller than wolves with print more narrow (2.5 to 3.5").

Fox
FRONT   REAR

Smallest in the group with print (2 to 3") and fuzzy around edges.

Dog
FRONT   REAR

Similar to wolf/coyote with thicker nails.

Feline

Cougar / Mountain Lion
FRONT   REAR

Largest in the group (greater than 3"). Size of domestic dog.

Lynx
FRONT   REAR

Same as cougar but smaller in size and not as defined due to fur around paws.

Bobcat
FRONT   REAR

Smaller tracks (2"). Often confused with coyote or fox but lacks nails. Round shape.

House Cat
FRONT   REAR

Small (1 to 1.5"). Similar to domestic dog, meander when walking.

Bird

Crow
Standard bird track: 3 forward, 1 rear. Print 2-2.5".

Grouse
Small ground birds with only 3 forward toes. Print 2" long.

Turkey
Similar to grouse but much larger prints (4") long.

Duck
Webbing gives its print distinctive shape.

Bear

Black Bear
FRONT   REAR

Has short claws and its toes spread out in a curve over its foot pad. Generally going to be smaller than grizzly bear paw.

Grizzly Bear
FRONT   REAR

Has long claws that extend out further from their toes. Its toes also are held closer together, forming almost a straight line above the foot pad.

Rodent

Beaver

FRONT   REAR
Webbed hind feet with 5 toes (4.5-7"). Sometime 4-toed prints.

Porcupine

FRONT   REAR
Usually only see pads in prints (1-2"). Pigeon-toed.

Muskrat

FRONT   REAR
Hand-like like raccoon but smaller (2.3").

Mouse

FRONT   REAR
Larger back feet (1.5 - 2"), smaller front feet (0.25-0.5").

Squirrel

FRONT   REAR
Larger back feet (1.5-2"), smaller front feet (1-1.5").

Hoof

Mountain Goat

FRONT   REAR
Have toes that spread when they step, creating a distinctive V shape at the top of their print.

Bighorn Sheep

FRONT   REAR
Similar to deer but with straighter edges and less pointed. More blocky and less shaped like a heart.

Wild Hog

FRONT   REAR
Often confused with deer but toes are wider, rounder and blunter and don't come to a point. Have dew claw that rests slightly outside print.

Reptile / Amphibian

Alligator

FRONT   REAR
Large feet with four toes on front prints and five toes on rear prints. Front are wide in heel, rear are longer, narrow and pointed heel.

Lizard

FRONT   REAR
Lightweight and don't leave much of a track. Might leave small scuff from feet and small tail drag.

Frog

FRONT   REAR
Have four bulbous toes in front and five in hind prints. Front toes point slightly inward producing a "K" shaped print, while rear toes slope upward and outward.

Other Common

Raccoon

FRONT   REAR
Five toes resembles hand of a baby. Front print smaller (1-3") with C-shaped heel pad. Rear print longer (1.5-4") heel pad.

Opossum

FRONT   REAR
Five fingers and human hand shape. Opposable thumbs on hind feet.

Rabbit

REAR
FRONT
Larger hind feet, smaller front feet. Hoppers producing a "Y" shaped track.

Skunk

FRONT   REAR
Five toes on their hind and front feet. Front and rear are approximately same size. Claws show up in many prints.

Otter

FRONT   REAR
Five toes and short claws give their prints a pointed look. Toes are partially webbed.

Armadillo

REAR
FRONT
Four long toe prints with sharp claw at tip. Front print show distinct "V" between middle toes.

Sketch / Notes

Sketch

_____
_____
_____
_____
_____
_____
_____
_____
_____
_____
_____

General

Date: _____   Location: _____

Environment: ◯ Mud   ◯ Snow   ◯ Soft Garden Soil   ◯ Sand

Time of Day: ◯ Morning   ◯ Midday   ◯ Evening   ◯ Time_____

Front Toes: ◯ Five   ◯ Four   ◯ Three   ◯ Two

Rear Toes: ◯ Five   ◯ Four   ◯ Three   ◯ Two

Track Symmetry: ◯ Symmetric   ◯ Asymmetric

Claws / Nails: ◯ Visible   ◯ Not Visible   Webbing: ◯ Yes   ◯ No

Surroundings: _____

Movement Pattern: ◯ Zig-Zaggler   ◯ Trot   ◯ Lope   ◯ Gallop

Notes: _____

Canine

Wolf

FRONT   REAR

Biggest in this group with a long (4") and wide print.

Coyote
FRONT   REAR

Slightly smaller than wolves with print more narrow (2.5 to 3.5").

Fox
FRONT   REAR

Smallest in the group with print (2 to 3") and fuzzy around edges.

Dog
FRONT   REAR

Similar to wolf/coyote with thicker nails.

Feline

Cougar / Mountain Lion

FRONT   REAR

Largest in the group (greater than 3"). Size of domestic dog.

Lynx

FRONT   REAR

Same as cougar but smaller in size and not as defined due to fur around paws.

Bobcat
FRONT   REAR

Smaller tracks (2"). Often confused with coyote or fox but lacks nails. Round shape.

House Cat
FRONT   REAR

Small (1 to 1.5"). Similar to domestic dog, meander when walking.

Bird

Crow

Standard bird track: 3 forward, 1 rear. Print 2-2.5".

Grouse

Small ground birds with only 3 forward toes. Print 2" long.

Turkey

Similar to grouse but much larger prints (4") long.

Duck

Webbing gives its print distinctive shape.

Bear

Black Bear

FRONT   REAR

Has short claws and its toes spread out in a curve over its foot pad. Generally going to be smaller than grizzly bear paw.

Grizzly Bear

FRONT   REAR

Has long claws that extend out further from their toes. Its toes also are held closer together, forming almost a straight line above the foot pad.

Beaver

FRONT   REAR

Webbed hind feet with 5 toes (4.5-7"). Sometime 4-toed prints.

Porcupine

FRONT   REAR

Usually only see pads in prints (1-2"). Pigeon-toed.

Muskrat

FRONT   REAR

Hand-like like raccoon but smaller (2.3").

Mouse

FRONT   REAR

Larger back feet (1.5 - 2"), smaller front feet (0.25-0.5").

Squirrel

FRONT   REAR

Larger back feet (1.5-2"), smaller front feet (1-1.5").

Mountain Goat

FRONT   REAR

Have toes that spread when they step, creating a distinctive V shape at the top of their print.

Bighorn Sheep

FRONT   REAR

Similar to deer but with straighter edges and less pointed. More blocky and less shaped like a heart.

Wild Hog

FRONT   REAR

Often confused with deer but toes are wider, rounder and blunter and don't come to a point. Have dew claw that rests slightly outside print.

Alligator

FRONT

REAR

Large feet with four toes on front prints and five toes on rear prints. Front are wide in heel, rear are longer, narrow and pointed heel.

Lizard

FRONT   REAR

Lightweight and don't leave much of a track. Might leave small scuff from feet and small tail drag.

Frog

FRONT   REAR

Have four bulbous toes in front and five in hind prints. Front toes point slightly inward producing a "K" shaped print, while rear toes slope upward and outward.

Raccoon

FRONT

REAR

Five toes resembles hand of a baby. Front print smaller (1-3") with C-shaped heel pad. Rear print longer (1.5-4") heel pad.

Opossum

FRONT   REAR

Five fingers and human hand shape. Opposable thumbs on hind feet.

Rabbit

REAR

FRONT

Larger hind feet, smaller front feet. Hoppers producing a "Y" shaped track.

Skunk

FRONT

REAR

Five toes on their hind and front feet. Front and rear are approximately same size. Claws show up in many prints.

Otter

FRONT   REAR

Five toes and short claws give their prints a pointed look. Toes are partially webbed.

Armadillo

REAR

FRONT

Four long toe prints with sharp claw at tip. Front print show distinct "V" between middle toes.

Sketch

_____
_____
_____
_____
_____
_____
_____
_____
_____
_____
_____

General

Date: _____ Location:_____

Environment: ◯ Mud ◯ Snow ◯ Soft Garden Soil ◯ Sand

Time of Day: ◯ Morning ◯ Midday ◯ Evening ◯ Time_____

Front Toes: ◯ Five ◯ Four ◯ Three ◯ Two

Rear Toes: ◯ Five ◯ Four ◯ Three ◯ Two

Track Symmetry: ◯ Symmetric ◯ Asymmetric

Claws / Nails: ◯ Visible ◯ Not Visible   Webbing: ◯ Yes ◯ No

Surroundings:_____

Movement Pattern: ◯ Zig-Zaggler ◯ Trot ◯ Lope ◯ Gallop

Notes:_____

Canine

Wolf	Coyote	Fox	Dog

FRONT REAR   FRONT REAR   FRONT REAR   FRONT REAR

Biggest in this group with a long (4") and wide print. | Slightly smaller than wolves with print more narrow (2.5 to 3.5"). | Smallest in the group with print (2 to 3") and fuzzy around edges. | Similar to wolf/coyote with thicker nails.

Feline

Cougar / Mountain Lion	Lynx	Bobcat	House Cat

FRONT REAR   FRONT REAR   FRONT REAR   FRONT REAR

Largest in the group (greater than 3"). Size of domestic dog. | Same as cougar but smaller in size and not as defined due to fur around paws. | Smaller tracks (2"). Often confused with coyote or fox but lacks nails. Round shape. | Small (1 to 1.5"). Similar to domestic dog, meander when walking.

Bird

Crow	Grouse	Turkey	Duck

Standard bird track: 3 forward, 1 rear. Print 2-2.5". | Small ground birds with only 3 forward toes. Print 2" long. | Similar to grouse but much larger prints (4") long. | Webbing gives its print distinctive shape.

Bear

Black Bear

Has short claws and its toes spread out in a curve over its foot pad. Generally going to be smaller than grizzly bear paw.

FRONT REAR

Grizzly Bear

Has long claws that extend out further from their toes. Its toes also are held closer together, forming almost a straight line above the foot pad.

FRONT REAR

Rodent

Beaver

FRONT   REAR
Webbed hind feet with 5 toes (4.5-7"). Sometime 4-toed prints.

Porcupine

FRONT REAR
Usually only see pads in prints (1-2"). Pigeon-toed.

Muskrat

FRONT   REAR
Hand-like like raccoon but smaller (2.3").

Mouse

FRONT REAR
Larger back feet (1.5 - 2"), smaller front feet (0.25-0.5").

Squirrel

FRONT   REAR
Larger back feet (1.5-2"), smaller front feet (1-1.5").

Hoof

Mountain Goat

FRONT   REAR
Have toes that spread when they step, creating a distinctive V shape at the top of their print.

Bighorn Sheep

FRONT   REAR
Similar to deer but with straighter edges and less pointed. More blocky and less shaped like a heart.

Wild Hog

FRONT   REAR
Often confused with deer but toes are wider, rounder and blunter and don't come to a point. Have dew claw that rests slightly outside print.

Reptile / Amphibian

Alligator

FRONT

REAR
Large feet with four toes on front prints and five toes on rear prints. Front are wide in heel, rear are longer, narrow and pointed heel.

Lizard

FRONT   REAR
Lightweight and don't leave much of a track. Might leave small scuff from feet and small tail drag.

Frog

FRONT   REAR
Have four bulbous toes in front and five in hind prints. Front toes point slightly inward producing a "K" shaped print, while rear toes slope upward and outward.

Other Common

Raccoon

FRONT

REAR
Five toes resembles hand of a baby. Front print smaller (1-3") with C-shaped heel pad. Rear print longer (1.5-4") heel pad.

Opossum

FRONT   REAR
Five fingers and human hand shape. Opposable thumbs on hind feet .

Rabbit
REAR

FRONT
Larger hind feet, smaller front feet. Hoppers producing a "Y" shaped track.

Skunk

FRONT   REAR
Five toes on their hind and front feet. Front and rear are approximately same size. Claws show up in many prints.

Otter

FRONT   REAR
Five toes and short claws give their prints a pointed look. Toes are partially webbed.

Armadillo
REAR
FRONT
Four long toe prints with sharp claw at tip. Front print show distinct "V" between middle toes.

Sketch / Notes

Sketch

_____
_____
_____
_____
_____
_____
_____
_____
_____
_____

General

Date: _____ Location: _____

Environment: ◯ Mud ◯ Snow ◯ Soft Garden Soil ◯ Sand

Time of Day: ◯ Morning ◯ Midday ◯ Evening ◯ Time _____

Front Toes: ◯ Five ◯ Four ◯ Three ◯ Two

Rear Toes: ◯ Five ◯ Four ◯ Three ◯ Two

Track Symmetry: ◯ Symmetric ◯ Asymmetric

Claws / Nails: ◯ Visible ◯ Not Visible   Webbing: ◯ Yes ◯ No

Surroundings: _____

Movement Pattern: ◯ Zig-Zaggler ◯ Trot ◯ Lope ◯ Gallop

Notes: _____

Canine

Wolf

FRONT   REAR

Biggest in this group with a long (4") and wide print.

Coyote
FRONT   REAR

Slightly smaller than wolves with print more narrow (2.5 to 3.5").

Fox

FRONT   REAR

Smallest in the group with print (2 to 3") and fuzzy around edges.

Dog

FRONT   REAR

Similar to wolf/coyote with thicker nails.

Feline

Cougar / Mountain Lion
FRONT   REAR

Largest in the group (greater than 3"). Size of domestic dog.

Lynx

FRONT   REAR

Same as cougar but smaller in size and not as defined due to fur around paws.

Bobcat

FRONT   REAR

Smaller tracks (2"). Often confused with coyote or fox but lacks nails. Round shape.

House Cat

FRONT   REAR

Small (1 to 1.5"). Similar to domestic dog, meander when walking.

Bird

Crow
Standard bird track: 3 forward, 1 rear. Print 2-2.5".

Grouse
Small ground birds with only 3 forward toes. Print 2" long.

Turkey
Similar to grouse but much larger prints (4") long.

Duck
Webbing gives its print distinctive shape.

Bear

Black Bear

FRONT   REAR

Has short claws and its toes spread out in a curve over its foot pad. Generally going to be smaller than grizzly bear paw.

Grizzly Bear

FRONT   REAR

Has long claws that extend out further from their toes. Its toes also are held closer together, forming almost a straight line above the foot pad.

Rodent

Beaver

FRONT REAR
Webbed hind feet with 5 toes (4.5-7"). Sometime 4-toed prints.

Porcupine

FRONT REAR
Usually only see pads in prints (1-2"). Pigeon-toed.

Muskrat

FRONT REAR
Hand-like like raccoon but smaller (2.3").

Mouse

FRONT REAR
Larger back feet (1.5 - 2"), smaller front feet (0.25-0.5").

Squirrel

FRONT REAR
Larger back feet (1.5-2"), smaller front feet (1-1.5").

Hoof

Mountain Goat

FRONT REAR
Have toes that spread when they step, creating a distinctive V shape at the top of their print.

Bighorn Sheep

FRONT REAR
Similar to deer but with straighter edges and less pointed. More blocky and less shaped like a heart.

Wild Hog

FRONT REAR
Often confused with deer but toes are wider, rounder and blunter and don't come to a point. Have dew claw that rests slightly outside print.

Reptile / Amphibian

Alligator

FRONT
REAR
Large feet with four toes on front prints and five toes on rear prints. Front are wide in heel, rear are longer, narrow and pointed heel.

Lizard

FRONT REAR
Lightweight and don't leave much of a track. Might leave small scuff from feet and small tail drag.

Frog

FRONT REAR
Have four bulbous toes in front and five in hind prints. Front toes point slightly inward producing a "K" shaped print, while rear toes slope upward and outward.

Other Common

Raccoon

FRONT
REAR
Five toes resembles hand of a baby. Front print smaller (1-3") with C-shaped heel pad. Rear print longer (1.5-4") heel pad.

Opossum

FRONT REAR
Five fingers and human hand shape. Opposable thumbs on hind feet.

Rabbit
REAR
FRONT
Larger hind feet, smaller front feet. Hoppers producing a "Y" shaped track.

Skunk

FRONT
REAR
Five toes on their hind and front feet. Front and rear are approximately same size. Claws show up in many prints.

Otter

FRONT REAR
Five toes and short claws give their prints a pointed look. Toes are partially webbed.

Armadillo
REAR
FRONT
Four long toe prints with sharp claw at tip. Front print show distinct "V" between middle toes.

Sketch

Sketch / Notes

General

Date: _____   Location: _____

Environment: ◯ Mud   ◯ Snow   ◯ Soft Garden Soil   ◯ Sand

Time of Day: ◯ Morning   ◯ Midday   ◯ Evening   ◯ Time _____

Front Toes: ◯ Five   ◯ Four   ◯ Three   ◯ Two

Rear Toes: ◯ Five   ◯ Four   ◯ Three   ◯ Two

Track Symmetry: ◯ Symmetric   ◯ Asymmetric

Claws / Nails: ◯ Visible   ◯ Not Visible   Webbing: ◯ Yes   ◯ No

Surroundings: _____

Movement Pattern: ◯ Zig-Zaggler   ◯ Trot   ◯ Lope   ◯ Gallop

Notes: _____

Canine

Wolf

FRONT   REAR

Biggest in this group with a long (4") and wide print.

Coyote

FRONT   REAR

Slightly smaller than wolves with print more narrow (2.5 to 3.5").

Fox

FRONT   REAR

Smallest in the group with print (2 to 3") and fuzzy around edges.

Dog

FRONT   REAR

Similar to wolf/coyote with thicker nails.

Feline

Cougar / Mountain Lion
FRONT   REAR

Largest in the group (greater than 3"). Size of domestic dog.

Lynx

FRONT   REAR

Same as cougar but smaller in size and not as defined due to fur around paws.

Bobcat

FRONT   REAR

Smaller tracks (2"). Often confused with coyote or fox but lacks nails. Round shape.

House Cat

FRONT   REAR

Small (1 to 1.5"). Similar to domestic dog, meander when walking.

Bird

Crow
FRONT
Standard bird track: 3 forward, 1 rear. Print 2-2.5".

Grouse

Small ground birds with only 3 forward toes. Print 2" long.

Turkey
Similar to grouse but much larger prints (4") long.

Duck
Webbing gives its print distinctive shape.

Bear

Black Bear

FRONT   REAR

Has short claws and its toes spread out in a curve over its foot pad. Generally going to be smaller than grizzly bear paw.

Grizzly Bear

FRONT   REAR

Has long claws that extend out further from their toes. Its toes also are held closer together, forming almost a straight line above the foot pad.

Beaver

FRONT   REAR

Webbed hind feet with 5 toes (4.5-7"). Sometime 4-toed prints.

Porcupine

FRONT REAR

Usually only see pads in prints (1-2"). Pigeon-toed.

Muskrat

FRONT   REAR

Hand-like like raccoon but smaller (2.3").

Mouse

FRONT   REAR

Larger back feet (1.5 - 2"), smaller front feet (0.25-0.5").

Squirrel

FRONT   REAR

Larger back feet (1.5-2"), smaller front feet (1-1.5").

Mountain Goat

FRONT   REAR

Have toes that spread when they step, creating a distinctive V shape at the top of their print.

Bighorn Sheep

FRONT   REAR

Similar to deer but with straighter edges and less pointed. More blocky and less shaped like a heart.

Wild Hog

FRONT   REAR

Often confused with deer but toes are wider, rounder and blunter and don't come to a point. Have dew claw that rests slightly outside print.

Alligator

FRONT

REAR

Large feet with four toes on front prints and five toes on rear prints. Front are wide in heel, rear are longer, narrow and pointed heel.

Lizard

FRONT   REAR

Lightweight and don't leave much of a track. Might leave small scuff from feet and small tail drag.

Frog

FRONT   REAR

Have four bulbous toes in front and five in hind prints. Front toes point slightly inward producing a "K" shaped print, while rear toes slope upward and outward.

Raccoon

FRONT

REAR

Five toes resembles hand of a baby. Front print smaller (1-3") with C-shaped heel pad. Rear print longer (1.5-4") heel pad.

Opossum

FRONT   REAR

Five fingers and human hand shape. Opposable thumbs on hind feet .

Rabbit

REAR

FRONT

Larger hind feet, smaller front feet. Hoppers producing a "Y" shaped track.

Skunk

FRONT

REAR

Five toes on their hind and front feet. Front and rear are approximately same size. Claws show up in many prints.

Otter

FRONT   REAR

Five toes and short claws give their prints a pointed look. Toes are partially webbed.

Armadillo

REAR

FRONT

Four long toe prints with sharp claw at tip. Front print show distinct "V" between middle toes.

Sketch

_____
_____
_____
_____
_____
_____
_____
_____
_____
_____
_____
_____

General

Date: _____ Location: _____

Environment: ◯ Mud ◯ Snow ◯ Soft Garden Soil ◯ Sand

Time of Day: ◯ Morning ◯ Midday ◯ Evening ◯ Time_____

Front Toes: ◯ Five ◯ Four ◯ Three ◯ Two

Rear Toes: ◯ Five ◯ Four ◯ Three ◯ Two

Track Symmetry: ◯ Symmetric ◯ Asymmetric

Claws / Nails: ◯ Visible ◯ Not Visible Webbing: ◯ Yes ◯ No

Surroundings: _____

Movement Pattern: ◯ Zig-Zaggler ◯ Trot ◯ Lope ◯ Gallop

Notes: _____

Canine

Wolf	Coyote	Fox	Dog
FRONT REAR	FRONT REAR	FRONT REAR	FRONT REAR
Biggest in this group with a long (4") and wide print.	Slightly smaller than wolves with print more narrow (2.5 to 3.5").	Smallest in the group with print (2 to 3") and fuzzy around edges.	Similar to wolf/coyote with thicker nails.

Feline

Cougar / Mountain Lion **Lynx** **Bobcat** **House Cat**

FRONT REAR   FRONT REAR   FRONT REAR   FRONT REAR

Largest in the group (greater than 3"). Size of domestic dog.

Same as cougar but smaller in size and not as defined due to fur around paws.

Smaller tracks (2"). Often confused with coyote or fox but lacks nails. Round shape.

Small (1 to 1.5"). Similar to domestic dog, meander when walking.

Bird

Crow **Grouse** **Turkey** **Duck**

Standard bird track: 3 forward, 1 rear. Print 2-2.5".

Small ground birds with only 3 forward toes. Print 2" long.

Similar to grouse but much larger prints (4") long.

Webbing gives its print distinctive shape.

Bear

Black Bear

FRONT REAR

Has short claws and its toes spread out in a curve over its foot pad. Generally going to be smaller than grizzly bear paw.

Grizzly Bear

FRONT REAR

Has long claws that extend out further from their toes. Its toes also are held closer together, forming almost a straight line above the foot pad.

Rodent

Beaver

FRONT   REAR
Webbed hind feet with 5 toes (4.5-7"). Sometime 4-toed prints.

Porcupine

FRONT   REAR
Usually only see pads in prints (1-2"). Pigeon-toed.

Muskrat

FRONT   REAR
Hand-like like raccoon but smaller (2.3").

Mouse

FRONT   REAR
Larger back feet (1.5 - 2"), smaller front feet (0.25-0.5").

Squirrel

FRONT   REAR
Larger back feet (1.5-2"), smaller front feet (1-1.5").

Hoof

Mountain Goat

FRONT   REAR
Have toes that spread when they step, creating a distinctive V shape at the top of their print.

Bighorn Sheep

FRONT   REAR
Similar to deer but with straighter edges and less pointed. More blocky and less shaped like a heart.

Wild Hog

FRONT   REAR
Often confused with deer but toes are wider, rounder and blunter and don't come to a point. Have dew claw that rests slightly outside print.

Reptile / Amphibian

Alligator

FRONT
REAR
Large feet with four toes on front prints and five toes on rear prints. Front are wide in heel, rear are longer, narrow and pointed heel.

Lizard

FRONT   REAR
Lightweight and don't leave much of a track. Might leave small scuff from feet and small tail drag.

Frog

FRONT   REAR
Have four bulbous toes in front and five in hind prints. Front toes point slightly inward producing a "K" shaped print, while rear toes slope upward and outward.

Other Common

Raccoon

FRONT
REAR
Five toes resembles hand of a baby. Front print smaller (1-3") with C-shaped heel pad. Rear print longer (1.5-4") heel pad.

Opossum

FRONT   REAR
Five fingers and human hand shape. Opposable thumbs on hind feet.

Rabbit
REAR

FRONT
Larger hind feet, smaller front feet. Hoppers producing a "Y" shaped track.

Skunk

FRONT   REAR
Five toes on their hind and front feet. Front and rear are approximately same size. Claws show up in many prints.

Otter

FRONT   REAR
Five toes and short claws give their prints a pointed look. Toes are partially webbed.

Armadillo
REAR

FRONT
Four long toe prints with sharp claw at tip. Front print show distinct "V" between middle toes.

Sketch

Sketch / Notes

_____
_____
_____
_____
_____
_____
_____
_____
_____
_____
_____

General

Date: _____ Location: _____

Environment: ○ Mud   ○ Snow   ○ Soft Garden Soil   ○ Sand

Time of Day: ○ Morning   ○ Midday   ○ Evening   ○ Time _____

Front Toes: ○ Five   ○ Four   ○ Three   ○ Two

Rear Toes: ○ Five   ○ Four   ○ Three   ○ Two

Track Symmetry: ○ Symmetric   ○ Asymmetric

Claws / Nails: ○ Visible   ○ Not Visible   Webbing: ○ Yes   ○ No

Surroundings: _____

Movement Pattern: ○ Zig-Zaggler   ○ Trot   ○ Lope   ○ Gallop

Notes: _____

Canine

Wolf

FRONT   REAR

Biggest in this group with a long (4") and wide print.

Coyote
FRONT   REAR

Slightly smaller than wolves with print more narrow (2.5 to 3.5").

Fox
FRONT   REAR

Smallest in the group with print (2 to 3") and fuzzy around edges.

Dog
FRONT   REAR

Similar to wolf/coyote with thicker nails.

Feline

Cougar / Mountain Lion
FRONT   REAR

Largest in the group (greater than 3"). Size of domestic dog.

Lynx
FRONT   REAR

Same as cougar but smaller in size and not as defined due to fur around paws.

Bobcat
FRONT   REAR

Smaller tracks (2"). Often confused with coyote or fox but lacks nails. Round shape.

House Cat
FRONT   REAR

Small (1 to 1.5"). Similar to domestic dog, meander when walking.

Bird

Crow

Standard bird track: 3 forward, 1 rear. Print 2-2.5".

Grouse

Small ground birds with only 3 forward toes. Print 2" long.

Turkey

Similar to grouse but much larger prints (4") long.

Duck

Webbing gives its print distinctive shape.

Bear

Black Bear

FRONT   REAR

Has short claws and its toes spread out in a curve over its foot pad. Generally going to be smaller than grizzly bear paw.

Grizzly Bear

FRONT   REAR

Has long claws that extend out further from their toes. Its toes also are held closer together, forming almost a straight line above the foot pad.

Beaver

FRONT   REAR

Webbed hind feet with 5 toes (4.5-7"). Sometime 4-toed prints.

Porcupine

FRONT   REAR

Usually only see pads in prints (1-2"). Pigeon-toed.

Muskrat

FRONT   REAR

Hand-like like raccoon but smaller (2.3").

Mouse

FRONT   REAR

Larger back feet (1.5 - 2"), smaller front feet (0.25-0.5").

Squirrel
FRONT   REAR

Larger back feet (1.5-2"), smaller front feet (1-1.5").

Mountain Goat

FRONT   REAR

Have toes that spread when they step, creating a distinctive V shape at the top of their print.

Bighorn Sheep

FRONT   REAR

Similar to deer but with straighter edges and less pointed. More blocky and less shaped like a heart.

Wild Hog

FRONT   REAR

Often confused with deer but toes are wider, rounder and blunter and don't come to a point. Have dew claw that rests slightly outside print.

Alligator

FRONT
REAR

Large feet with four toes on front prints and five toes on rear prints. Front are wide in heel, rear are longer, narrow and pointed heel.

Lizard

FRONT   REAR

Lightweight and don't leave much of a track. Might leave small scuff from feet and small tail drag.

Frog

FRONT   REAR

Have four bulbous toes in front and five in rear prints. Front toes point slightly inward producing a "K" shaped print, while rear toes slope upward and outward.

Raccoon

FRONT
REAR

Five toes resembles hand of a baby. Front print smaller (1-3") with C-shaped heel pad. Rear print longer (1.5-4") heel pad.

Opossum

FRONT   REAR

Five fingers and human hand shape. Opposable thumbs on hind feet.

Rabbit
REAR

FRONT

Larger hind feet, smaller front feet. Hoppers producing a "Y" shaped track.

Skunk

FRONT   REAR

Five toes on their hind and front feet. Front and rear are approximately same size. Claws show up in many prints.

Otter

FRONT   REAR

Five toes and short claws give their prints a pointed look. Toes are partially webbed.

Armadillo
REAR

FRONT

Four long toe prints with sharp claw at tip. Front print show distinct "V" between middle toes.

Sketch

General

Date: _____ Location: _____

Environment: ○ Mud ○ Snow ○ Soft Garden Soil ○ Sand

Time of Day: ○ Morning ○ Midday ○ Evening ○ Time _____

Front Toes: ○ Five ○ Four ○ Three ○ Two

Rear Toes: ○ Five ○ Four ○ Three ○ Two

Track Symmetry: ○ Symmetric ○ Asymmetric

Claws / Nails: ○ Visible ○ Not Visible   Webbing: ○ Yes ○ No

Surroundings: _____

Movement Pattern: ○ Zig-Zaggler   ○ Trot   ○ Lope   ○ Gallop

Notes: _____

Canine

Wolf

FRONT REAR

Biggest in this group with a long (4") and wide print.

Coyote
FRONT REAR

Slightly smaller than wolves with print more narrow (2.5 to 3.5").

Fox
FRONT REAR

Smallest in the group with print (2 to 3") and fuzzy around edges.

Dog
FRONT REAR

Similar to wolf/coyote with thicker nails.

Feline

Cougar / Mountain Lion
FRONT REAR

Largest in the group (greater than 3"). Size of domestic dog.

Lynx
FRONT REAR

Same as cougar but smaller in size and not as defined due to fur around paws.

Bobcat
FRONT REAR

Smaller tracks (2"). Often confused with coyote or fox but lacks nails. Round shape.

House Cat
FRONT REAR

Small (1 to 1.5"). Similar to domestic dog, meander when walking.

Bird

Crow

Standard bird track: 3 forward, 1 rear. Print 2-2.5".

Grouse

Small ground birds with only 3 forward toes. Print 2" long.

Turkey

Similar to grouse but much larger prints (4") long.

Duck

Webbing gives its print distinctive shape.

Bear

Black Bear

FRONT REAR

Has short claws and its toes spread out in a curve over its foot pad. Generally going to be smaller than grizzly bear paw.

Grizzly Bear

FRONT REAR

Has long claws that extend out further from their toes. Its toes also are held closer together, forming almost a straight line above the foot pad.

Rodent

Beaver

FRONT   REAR
Webbed hind feet with 5 toes (4.5-7"). Sometime 4-toed prints.

Porcupine

FRONT   REAR
Usually only see pads in prints (1-2"). Pigeon-toed.

Muskrat

FRONT   REAR
Hand-like like raccoon but smaller (2.3").

Mouse

FRONT   REAR
Larger back feet (1.5 - 2"), smaller front feet (0.25-0.5").

Squirrel

FRONT   REAR
Larger back feet (1.5-2"), smaller front feet (1-1.5").

Hoof

Mountain Goat

FRONT   REAR
Have toes that spread when they step, creating a distinctive V shape at the top of their print.

Bighorn Sheep

FRONT   REAR
Similar to deer but with straighter edges and less pointed. More blocky and less shaped like a heart.

Wild Hog

FRONT   REAR
Often confused with deer but toes are wider, rounder and blunter and don't come to a point. Have dew claw that rests slightly outside print.

Reptile / Amphibian

Alligator

FRONT
REAR
Large feet with four toes on front prints and five toes on rear prints. Front are wide in heel, rear are longer, narrow and pointed heel.

Lizard

FRONT   REAR
Lightweight and don't leave much of a track. Might leave small scuff from feet and small tail drag.

Frog
FRONT   REAR
Have four bulbous toes in front and five in hind prints. Front toes point slightly inward producing a "K" shaped print, while rear toes slope upward and outward.

Other Common

Raccoon

FRONT
REAR
Five toes resembles hand of a baby. Front print smaller (1-3") with C-shaped heel pad. Rear print longer (1.5-4") heel pad.

Opossum

FRONT   REAR
Five fingers and human hand shape. Opposable thumbs on hind feet.

Rabbit
REAR

FRONT
Larger hind feet, smaller front feet. Hoppers producing a "Y" shaped track.

Skunk

FRONT
REAR
Five toes on their hind and front feet. Front and rear are approximately same size. Claws show up in many prints.

Otter

FRONT   REAR
Five toes and short claws give their prints a pointed look. Toes are partially webbed.

Armadillo
REAR

FRONT
Four long toe prints with sharp claw at tip. Front print show distinct "V" between middle toes.

Sketch / Notes

Sketch

_____
_____
_____
_____
_____
_____
_____
_____
_____
_____
_____

General

Date: _____ Location: _____

Environment: ◯ Mud ◯ Snow ◯ Soft Garden Soil ◯ Sand

Time of Day: ◯ Morning ◯ Midday ◯ Evening ◯ Time_____

Front Toes: ◯ Five ◯ Four ◯ Three ◯ Two

Rear Toes: ◯ Five ◯ Four ◯ Three ◯ Two

Track Symmetry: ◯ Symmetric ◯ Asymmetric

Claws / Nails: ◯ Visible ◯ Not Visible Webbing: ◯ Yes ◯ No

Surroundings: _____

Movement Pattern: ◯ Zig-Zaggler ◯ Trot ◯ Lope ◯ Gallop

Notes: _____

Canine

Wolf

FRONT REAR

Biggest in this group with a long (4") and wide print.

Coyote
FRONT REAR

Slightly smaller than wolves with print more narrow (2.5 to 3.5").

Fox
FRONT REAR

Smallest in the group with print (2 to 3") and fuzzy around edges.

Dog
FRONT REAR

Similar to wolf/coyote with thicker nails.

Feline

Cougar / Mountain Lion

FRONT REAR

Largest in the group (greater than 3"). Size of domestic dog.

Lynx
FRONT REAR

Same as cougar but smaller in size and not as defined due to fur around paws.

Bobcat

FRONT REAR

Smaller tracks (2"). Often confused with coyote or fox but lacks nails. Round shape.

House Cat

FRONT REAR

Small (1 to 1.5"). Similar to domestic dog, meander when walking.

Bird

Crow

Standard bird track: 3 forward, 1 rear. Print 2-2.5".

Grouse

Small ground birds with only 3 forward toes. Print 2" long.

Turkey

Similar to grouse but much larger prints (4") long.

Duck

Webbing gives its print distinctive shape.

Bear

Black Bear

FRONT REAR

Has short claws and its toes spread out in a curve over its foot pad. Generally going to be smaller than grizzly bear paw.

Grizzly Bear
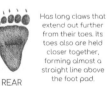
FRONT REAR

Has long claws that extend out further from their toes. Its toes also are held closer together, forming almost a straight line above the foot pad.

Beaver

FRONT   REAR

Webbed hind feet with 5 toes (4.5-7"). Sometime 4-toed prints.

Porcupine

FRONT REAR

Usually only see pads in prints (1-2"). Pigeon-toed.

Muskrat

FRONT   REAR

Hand-like like raccoon but smaller (2.3").

Mouse

FRONT REAR

Larger back feet (1.5 - 2"), smaller front feet (0.25-0.5").

Squirrel

FRONT   REAR

Larger back feet (1.5-2"), smaller front feet (1-1.5").

Mountain Goat

FRONT   REAR

Have toes that spread when they step, creating a distinctive V shape at the top of their print.

Bighorn Sheep

FRONT   REAR

Similar to deer but with straighter edges and less pointed. More blocky and less shaped like a heart.

Wild Hog

FRONT   REAR

Often confused with deer but toes are wider, rounder and blunter and don't come to a point. Have dew claw that rests slightly outside print.

Alligator

FRONT

REAR

Large feet with four toes on front prints and five toes on rear prints. Front are wide in heel, rear are longer, narrow and pointed heel.

Lizard

FRONT   REAR

Lightweight and don't leave much of a track. Might leave small scuff from feet and small tail drag.

Frog

FRONT   REAR

Have four bulbous toes in front and five in hind prints. Front toes point slightly inward producing a "K" shaped print, while rear toes slope upward and outward.

Raccoon

FRONT

REAR

Five toes resembles hand of a baby. Front print smaller (1-3") with C-shaped heel pad. Rear print longer (1.5-4") heel pad.

Opossum

FRONT   REAR

Five fingers and human hand shape. Opposable thumbs on hind feet.

Rabbit

REAR

FRONT

Larger hind feet, smaller front feet. Hoppers producing a "Y" shaped track.

Skunk

FRONT

REAR

Five toes on their hind and front feet. Front and rear are approximately same size. Claws show up in many prints.

Otter

FRONT   REAR

Five toes and short claws give their prints a pointed look. Toes are partially webbed.

Armadillo

REAR

FRONT

Four long toe prints with sharp claw at tip. Front print show distinct "V" between middle toes.

Sketch

General

Date: _____   Location: _____

Environment: ○ Mud   ○ Snow   ○ Soft Garden Soil   ○ Sand

Time of Day: ○ Morning   ○ Midday   ○ Evening   ○ Time_____

Front Toes: ○ Five   ○ Four   ○ Three   ○ Two

Rear Toes: ○ Five   ○ Four   ○ Three   ○ Two

Track Symmetry: ○ Symmetric   ○ Asymmetric

Claws / Nails: ○ Visible   ○ Not Visible   Webbing: ○ Yes   ○ No

Surroundings: _____

Movement Pattern: ○ Zig-Zaggler   ○ Trot   ○ Lope   ○ Gallop

Notes: _____

Canine

Wolf

FRONT   REAR

Biggest in this group with a long (4") and wide print.

Coyote
FRONT   REAR

Slightly smaller than wolves with print more narrow (2.5 to 3.5").

Fox
FRONT   REAR

Smallest in the group with print (2 to 3") and fuzzy around edges.

Dog
FRONT   REAR

Similar to wolf/coyote with thicker nails.

Feline

Cougar / Mountain Lion

FRONT   REAR

Largest in the group (greater than 3"). Size of domestic dog.

Lynx
FRONT   REAR

Same as cougar but smaller in size and not as defined due to fur around paws.

Bobcat
FRONT   REAR

Smaller tracks (2"). Often confused with coyote or fox but lacks nails. Round shape.

House Cat
FRONT   REAR

Small (1 to 1.5"). Similar to domestic dog, meander when walking.

Bird

Crow

Standard bird track: 3 forward, 1 rear. Print 2-2.5".

Grouse

Small ground birds with only 3 forward toes. Print 2" long.

Turkey

Similar to grouse but much larger prints (4") long.

Duck

Webbing gives its print distinctive shape.

Bear

Black Bear

FRONT   REAR

Has short claws and its toes spread out in a curve over its foot pad. Generally going to be smaller than grizzly bear paw.

Grizzly Bear

FRONT   REAR

Has long claws that extend out further from their toes. Its toes also are held closer together, forming almost a straight line above the foot pad.

Rodent

Beaver

FRONT   REAR
Webbed hind feet with 5 toes (4.5-7'). Sometime 4-toed prints.

Porcupine

FRONT   REAR
Usually only see pads in prints (1-2'). Pigeon-toed.

Muskrat

FRONT   REAR
Hand-like like raccoon but smaller (2.3').

Mouse
FRONT   REAR
Larger back feet (1.5 - 2'), smaller front feet (0.25-0.5').

Squirrel

FRONT   REAR
Larger back feet (1.5-2'), smaller front feet (1-1.5').

Hoof

Mountain Goat

FRONT   REAR
Have toes that spread when they step, creating a distinctive V shape at the top of their print.

Bighorn Sheep

FRONT   REAR
Similar to deer but with straighter edges and less pointed. More blocky and less shaped like a heart.

Wild Hog

FRONT   REAR
Often confused with deer but toes are wider, rounder and blunter and don't come to a point. Have dew claw that rests slightly outside print.

Reptile / Amphibian

Alligator

FRONT
REAR
Large feet with four toes on front prints and five toes on rear prints. Front are wide in heel, rear are longer, narrow and pointed heel.

Lizard

FRONT   REAR
Lightweight and don't leave much of a track. Might leave small scuff from feet and small tail drag.

Frog

FRONT   REAR
Have four bulbous toes in front and five in hind prints. Front toes point slightly inward producing a "K" shaped print, while rear toes slope upward and outward.

Other Common

Raccoon

FRONT
REAR
Five toes resembles hand of a baby. Front print smaller (1-3') with C-shaped heel pad. Rear print longer (1.5-4') heel pad.

Opossum

FRONT   REAR
Five fingers and human hand shape. Opposable thumbs on hind feet .

Rabbit

REAR
FRONT
Larger hind feet, smaller front feet. Hoppers producing a 'Y' shaped track.

Skunk

FRONT
REAR
Five toes on their hind and front feet. Front and rear are approximately same size. Claws show up in many prints.

Otter

FRONT   REAR
Five toes and short claws give their prints a pointed look. Toes are partially webbed.

Armadillo

REAR
FRONT
Four long toe prints with sharp claw at tip. Front print show distinct 'V' between middle toes.

Sketch

Sketch / Notes

_____
_____
_____
_____
_____
_____
_____
_____
_____
_____
_____

General

Date: _____ Location: _____

Environment: ⬭ Mud ⬭ Snow ⬭ Soft Garden Soil ⬭ Sand

Time of Day: ⬭ Morning ⬭ Midday ⬭ Evening ⬭ Time_____

Front Toes: ⬭ Five ⬭ Four ⬭ Three ⬭ Two

Rear Toes: ⬭ Five ⬭ Four ⬭ Three ⬭ Two

Track Symmetry: ⬭ Symmetric ⬭ Asymmetric

Claws / Nails: ⬭ Visible ⬭ Not Visible Webbing: ⬭ Yes ⬭ No

Surroundings: _____

Movement Pattern: ⬭ Zig-Zaggler ⬭ Trot ⬭ Lope ⬭ Gallop

Notes: _____

Canine

Wolf

FRONT REAR

Biggest in this group with a long (4") and wide print.

Coyote
FRONT REAR

Slightly smaller than wolves with print more narrow (2.5 to 3.5").

Fox

FRONT REAR

Smallest in the group with print (2 to 3") and fuzzy around edges.

Dog

FRONT REAR

Similar to wolf/coyote with thicker nails.

Feline

Cougar / Mountain Lion

FRONT REAR

Largest in the group (greater than 3"). Size of domestic dog.

Lynx

FRONT REAR

Same as cougar but smaller in size and not as defined due to fur around paws.

Bobcat

FRONT REAR

Smaller tracks (2"). Often confused with coyote or fox but lacks nails. Round shape.

House Cat

FRONT REAR

Small (1 to 1.5"). Similar to domestic dog, meander when walking.

Bird

Crow

Standard bird track: 3 forward, 1 rear. Print 2-2.5".

Grouse

Small ground birds with only 3 forward toes. Print 2" long.

Turkey

Similar to grouse but much larger prints (4") long.

Duck

Webbing gives its print distinctive shape.

Bear

Black Bear

FRONT REAR

Has short claws and its toes spread out in a curve over its foot pad. Generally going to be smaller than grizzly bear paw.

Grizzly Bear
FRONT REAR

Has long claws that extend out further from their toes. Its toes also are held closer together, forming almost a straight line above the foot pad.

Rodent

Beaver

FRONT   REAR
Webbed hind feet with 5 toes (4.5-7"). Sometime 4-toed prints.

Porcupine

FRONT   REAR
Usually only see pads in prints (1-2"). Pigeon-toed.

Muskrat

FRONT   REAR
Hand-like like raccoon but smaller (2,3").

Mouse

FRONT   REAR
Larger back feet (1.5 - 2"), smaller front feet (0,25-0.5").

Squirrel

FRONT   REAR
Larger back feet (1.5-2"), smaller front feet (1-1.5").

Hoof

Mountain Goat

FRONT   REAR
Have toes that spread when they step, creating a distinctive V shape at the top of their print.

Bighorn Sheep

FRONT   REAR
Similar to deer but with straighter edges and less pointed. More blocky and less shaped like a heart.

Wild Hog

FRONT   REAR
Often confused with deer but toes are wider, rounder and blunter and don't come to a point. Have dew claw that rests slightly outside print.

Reptile / Amphibian

Alligator

FRONT
REAR
Large feet with four toes on front prints and five toes on rear prints. Front are wide in heel, rear are longer, narrow and pointed heel.

Lizard

FRONT   REAR
Lightweight and don't leave much of a track. Might leave small scuff from feet and small tail drag.

Frog

FRONT   REAR
Have four bulbous toes in front and five in hind prints. Front toes point slightly inward producing a "K" shaped print, while rear toes slope upward and outward.

Other Common

Raccoon

FRONT
REAR
Five toes resembles hand of a baby. Front print smaller (1-3") with C-shaped heel pad. Rear print longer (1.5-4") heel pad.

Opossum

FRONT   REAR
Five fingers and human hand shape. Opposable thumbs on hind feet.

Rabbit

REAR
FRONT
Larger hind feet, smaller front feet. Hoppers producing a "Y" shaped track.

Skunk

FRONT
REAR
Five toes on their hind and front feet. Front and rear are approximately same size. Claws show up in many prints.

Otter

FRONT   REAR
Five toes and short claws give their prints a pointed look. Toes are partially webbed.

Armadillo

REAR
FRONT
Four long toe prints with sharp claw at tip. Front print show distinct "V" between middle toes.

Sketch

Sketch / Notes

_____
_____
_____
_____
_____
_____
_____
_____
_____
_____
_____

General

Date: _____ Location: _____

Environment: ○ Mud ○ Snow ○ Soft Garden Soil ○ Sand

Time of Day: ○ Morning ○ Midday ○ Evening ○ Time _____

Front Toes: ○ Five ○ Four ○ Three ○ Two

Rear Toes: ○ Five ○ Four ○ Three ○ Two

Track Symmetry: ○ Symmetric ○ Asymmetric

Claws / Nails: ○ Visible ○ Not Visible   Webbing: ○ Yes ○ No

Surroundings: _____

Movement Pattern: ○ Zig-Zaggler ○ Trot ○ Lope ○ Gallop

Notes: _____

Canine

Wolf	Coyote	Fox	Dog
FRONT REAR	FRONT REAR	FRONT REAR	FRONT REAR
Biggest in this group with a long (4") and wide print.	Slightly smaller than wolves with print more narrow (2.5 to 3.5").	Smallest in the group with print (2 to 3") and fuzzy around edges.	Similar to wolf/coyote with thicker nails.

Feline

Cougar / Mountain Lion	Lynx	Bobcat	House Cat
FRONT REAR	FRONT REAR	FRONT REAR	FRONT REAR
Largest in the group (greater than 3"). Size of domestic dog.	Same as cougar but smaller in size and not as defined due to fur around paws.	Smaller tracks (2"). Often confused with coyote or fox but lacks nails. Round shape.	Small (1 to 1.5"). Similar to domestic dog, meander when walking.

Bird

Crow	Grouse	Turkey	Duck
Standard bird track: 3 forward, 1 rear. Print 2-2.5".	Small ground birds with only 3 forward toes. Print 2" long.	Similar to grouse but much larger prints (4") long.	Webbing gives its print distinctive shape.

Bear

Black Bear
FRONT REAR

Has short claws and its toes spread out in a curve over its foot pad. Generally going to be smaller than grizzly bear paw.

Grizzly Bear
FRONT REAR

Has long claws that extend out further from their toes. Its toes also are held closer together, forming almost a straight line above the foot pad.

Rodent

Beaver

FRONT   REAR
Webbed hind feet with 5 toes (4.5-7"). Sometime 4-toed prints.

Porcupine

FRONT   REAR
Usually only see pads in prints (1-2"). Pigeon-toed.

Muskrat

FRONT   REAR
Hand-like like raccoon but smaller (2.3").

Mouse

FRONT   REAR
Larger back feet (1.5 - 2"), smaller front feet (0.25-0.5").

Squirrel

FRONT   REAR
Larger back feet (1.5-2"), smaller front feet (1-1.5").

Hoof

Mountain Goat

FRONT   REAR
Have toes that spread when they step, creating a distinctive V shape at the top of their print.

Bighorn Sheep

FRONT   REAR
Similar to deer but with straighter edges and less pointed. More blocky and less shaped like a heart.

Wild Hog

FRONT   REAR
Often confused with deer but toes are wider, rounder and blunter and don't come to a point. Have dew claw that rests slightly outside print.

Reptile / Amphibian

Alligator

FRONT
REAR
Large feet with four toes on front prints and five toes on rear prints. Front are wide in heel, rear are longer, narrow and pointed heel.

Lizard

FRONT   REAR
Lightweight and don't leave much of a track. Might leave small scuff from feet and small tail drag.

Frog

FRONT   REAR
Have four bulbous toes in front and five in hind prints. Front toes point slightly inward producing a "K" shaped print, while rear toes slope upward and outward.

Other Common

Raccoon

FRONT
REAR
Five toes resembles hand of a baby. Front print smaller (1-3") with C-shaped heel pad. Rear print longer (1.5-4") heel pad.

Opossum

FRONT   REAR
Five fingers and human hand shape. Opposable thumbs on hind feet.

Rabbit
REAR

FRONT
Larger hind feet, smaller front feet. Hoppers producing a "Y" shaped track.

Skunk

FRONT   REAR
Five toes on their hind and front feet. Front and rear are approximately same size. Claws show up in many prints.

Otter

FRONT   REAR
Five toes and short claws give their prints a pointed look. Toes are partially webbed.

Armadillo
REAR

FRONT
Four long toe prints with sharp claw at tip. Front print show distinct "V" between middle toes.

Sketch

Sketch / Notes

_____
_____
_____
_____
_____
_____
_____
_____
_____
_____
_____
_____

General

Date: _____ Location: _____

Environment: ⬭ Mud ⬭ Snow ⬭ Soft Garden Soil ⬭ Sand

Time of Day: ⬭ Morning ⬭ Midday ⬭ Evening ⬭ Time _____

Front Toes: ⬭ Five ⬭ Four ⬭ Three ⬭ Two

Rear Toes: ⬭ Five ⬭ Four ⬭ Three ⬭ Two

Track Symmetry: ⬭ Symmetric ⬭ Asymmetric

Claws / Nails: ⬭ Visible ⬭ Not Visible   Webbing: ⬭ Yes ⬭ No

Surroundings: _____

Movement Pattern: ⬭ Zig-Zaggler ⬭ Trot ⬭ Lope ⬭ Gallop

Notes: _____

Canine

Wolf
FRONT   REAR

Biggest in this group with a long (4") and wide print.

Coyote
FRONT   REAR

Slightly smaller than wolves with print more narrow (2.5 to 3.5").

Fox
FRONT   REAR

Smallest in the group with print (2 to 3") and fuzzy around edges.

Dog
FRONT   REAR

Similar to wolf/coyote with thicker nails.

Feline

Cougar / Mountain Lion
FRONT   REAR

Largest in the group (greater than 3"). Size of domestic dog.

Lynx
FRONT   REAR

Same as cougar but smaller in size and not as defined due to fur around paws.

Bobcat
FRONT   REAR

Smaller tracks (2"). Often confused with coyote or fox but lacks nails. Round shape.

House Cat
FRONT   REAR

Small (1 to 1.5"). Similar to domestic dog, meander when walking.

Bird

Crow

Standard bird track: 3 forward, 1 rear. Print 2-2.5".

Grouse

Small ground birds with only 3 forward toes. Print 2" long.

Turkey

Similar to grouse but much larger prints (4") long.

Duck

Webbing gives its print distinctive shape.

Bear

Black Bear
FRONT   REAR

Has short claws and its toes spread out in a curve over its foot pad. Generally going to be smaller than grizzly bear paw.

Grizzly Bear
FRONT   REAR

Has long claws that extend out further from their toes. Its toes also are held closer together, forming almost a straight line above the foot pad.

Rodent

Beaver

FRONT REAR
Webbed hind feet with 5 toes (4.5-7"). Sometime 4-toed prints.

Porcupine

FRONT REAR
Usually only see pads in prints (1-2"). Pigeon-toed.

Muskrat

FRONT REAR
Hand-like like smaller (2.3").

Mouse

FRONT REAR
Larger back feet (1.5 - 2"), smaller front feet (0.25-0.5").

Squirrel

FRONT REAR
Larger back feet (1.5-2"), smaller front feet (1-1.5").

Hoof

Mountain Goat

FRONT REAR
Have toes that spread when they step, creating a distinctive V shape at the top of their print.

Bighorn Sheep

FRONT REAR
Similar to deer but with straighter edges and less pointed. More blocky and less shaped like a heart.

Wild Hog

FRONT REAR
Often confused with deer but toes are wider, rounder and blunter and don't come to a point. Have dew claw that rests slightly outside print.

Reptile / Amphibian

Alligator

FRONT REAR
Large feet with four toes on front prints and five toes on rear prints. Front are wide in rear, rear are longer, narrow and pointed heel.

Lizard

FRONT REAR
Lightweight and don't leave much of a track. Might leave small scuff from feet and small tail drag.

Frog

FRONT REAR
Have four bulbous toes in front and five in hind prints. Front toes point slightly inward producing a "K" shaped print, while rear toes slope upward and outward.

Other Common

Raccoon

FRONT REAR
Five toes resembles hand of a baby. Front print smaller (1-3") with C-shaped heel pad. Rear print longer (1.5-4") heel pad.

Opossum

FRONT REAR
Five fingers and human hand shape. Opposable thumbs on hind feet.

Rabbit

REAR
FRONT
Larger hind feet, smaller front feet. Hoppers producing a "Y" shaped track.

Skunk

FRONT REAR
Five toes on their hind and front feet. Front and rear are approximately same size. Claws show up in many prints.

Otter

FRONT REAR
Five toes and short claws give their prints a pointed look. Toes are partially webbed.

Armadillo

REAR
FRONT
Four long toe prints with sharp claw at tip. Front print show distinct "V" between middle toes.

Sketch / Notes

Sketch

_____
_____
_____
_____
_____
_____
_____
_____
_____
_____
_____

General

Date: _____ Location: _____

Environment: ⬭ Mud ⬭ Snow ⬭ Soft Garden Soil ⬭ Sand

Time of Day: ⬭ Morning ⬭ Midday ⬭ Evening ⬭ Time_____

Front Toes: ⬭ Five ⬭ Four ⬭ Three ⬭ Two

Rear Toes: ⬭ Five ⬭ Four ⬭ Three ⬭ Two

Track Symmetry: ⬭ Symmetric ⬭ Asymmetric

Claws / Nails: ⬭ Visible ⬭ Not Visible   Webbing: ⬭ Yes ⬭ No

Surroundings: _____

Movement Pattern: ⬭ Zig-Zaggler ⬭ Trot ⬭ Lope ⬭ Gallop

Notes: _____

Canine

Wolf

FRONT   REAR

Biggest in this group with a long (4") and wide print.

Coyote
FRONT   REAR

Slightly smaller than wolves with print more narrow (2.5 to 3.5").

Fox
FRONT   REAR

Smallest in the group with print (2 to 3") and fuzzy around edges.

Dog
FRONT   REAR

Similar to wolf/coyote with thicker nails.

Feline

Cougar / Mountain Lion

FRONT   REAR

Largest in the group (greater than 3"). Size of domestic dog.

Lynx
FRONT   REAR

Same as cougar but smaller in size and not as defined due to fur around paws.

Bobcat
FRONT   REAR

Smaller tracks (2"). Often confused with coyote or fox but lacks nails. Round shape.

House Cat
FRONT   REAR

Small (1 to 1.5"). Similar to domestic dog, meander when walking.

Bird

Crow

Standard bird track: 3 forward, 1 rear. Print 2-2.5".

Grouse
Small ground birds with only 3 forward toes. Print 2" long.

Turkey
Similar to grouse but much larger prints (4") long.

Duck
Webbing gives its print distinctive shape.

Bear

Black Bear

FRONT   REAR

Has short claws and its toes spread out in a curve over its foot pad. Generally going to be smaller than grizzly bear paw.

Grizzly Bear
FRONT   REAR

Has long claws that extend out further from their toes. Its toes also are held closer together, forming almost a straight line above the foot pad.

Rodent

Beaver

FRONT   REAR
Webbed hind feet with 5 toes (4.5-7"). Sometime 4-toed prints.

Porcupine

FRONT   REAR
Usually only see pads in prints (1-2"). Pigeon-toed.

Muskrat

FRONT   REAR
Hand-like like raccoon but smaller (2.3").

Mouse

FRONT   REAR
Larger back feet (1.5 - 2"), smaller front feet (0.25-0.5").

Squirrel

FRONT   REAR
Larger back feet (1.5-2"), smaller front feet (1-1.5").

Hoof

Mountain Goat

FRONT   REAR
Have toes that spread when they step, creating a distinctive V shape at the top of their print.

Bighorn Sheep

FRONT   REAR
Similar to deer but with straighter edges and less pointed. More blocky and less shaped like a heart.

Wild Hog

FRONT   REAR
Often confused with deer but toes are wider, rounder and blunter and don't come to a point. Have dew claw that rests slightly outside print.

Reptile / Amphibian

Alligator

FRONT

REAR
Large feet with four toes on front prints and five toes on rear prints. Front are wide in heel, rear are longer, narrow and pointed heel.

Lizard

FRONT   REAR
Lightweight and don't leave much of a track. Might leave small scuff from feet and small tail drag.

Frog

FRONT   REAR
Have four bulbous toes in front and five in hind prints. Front toes point slightly inward producing a "K" shaped print, while rear toes slope upward and outward.

Other Common

Raccoon

FRONT

REAR
Five toes resembles hand of a baby. Front print smaller (1-3") with C-shaped heel pad. Rear print longer (1.5-4") heel pad.

Opossum

FRONT   REAR
Five fingers and human hand shape. Opposable thumbs on hind feet.

Rabbit
REAR

FRONT
Larger hind feet, smaller front feet. Hoppers producing a "Y" shaped track.

Skunk

FRONT

REAR
Five toes on their hind and front feet. Front and rear are approximately same size. Claws show up in many prints.

Otter

FRONT   REAR
Five toes and short claws give their prints a pointed look. Toes are partially webbed.

Armadillo
REAR

FRONT
Four long toe prints with sharp claw at tip. Front print show distinct "V" between middle toes.

Sketch

_____
_____
_____
_____
_____
_____
_____
_____
_____
_____
_____
_____

Sketch / Notes

General

Date: _____ Location: _____

Environment: ○ Mud ○ Snow ○ Soft Garden Soil ○ Sand

Time of Day: ○ Morning ○ Midday ○ Evening ○ Time _____

Front Toes: ○ Five ○ Four ○ Three ○ Two

Rear Toes: ○ Five ○ Four ○ Three ○ Two

Track Symmetry: ○ Symmetric ○ Asymmetric

Claws / Nails: ○ Visible ○ Not Visible Webbing: ○ Yes ○ No

Surroundings: _____

Movement Pattern: ○ Zig-Zaggler ○ Trot ○ Lope ○ Gallop

Notes: _____

Canine

Wolf

FRONT REAR

Biggest in this group with a long (4") and wide print.

Coyote
FRONT REAR

Slightly smaller than wolves with print more narrow (2.5 to 3.5").

Fox

FRONT REAR

Smallest in the group with print (2 to 3") and fuzzy around edges.

Dog

FRONT REAR

Similar to wolf/coyote with thicker nails.

Feline

Cougar / Mountain Lion

FRONT REAR

Largest in the group (greater than 3"). Size of domestic dog.

Lynx

FRONT REAR

Same as cougar but smaller in size and not as defined due to fur around paws.

Bobcat

FRONT REAR

Smaller tracks (2"). Often confused with coyote or fox but lacks nails. Round shape.

House Cat

FRONT REAR

Small (1 to 1.5"). Similar to domestic dog, meander when walking.

Bird

Crow
Standard bird track: 3 forward, 1 rear. Print 2-2.5".

Grouse
Small ground birds with only 3 forward toes. Print 2" long.

Turkey
Similar to grouse but much larger prints (4") long.

Duck
Webbing gives its print distinctive shape.

Bear

Black Bear

FRONT REAR

Has short claws and its toes spread out in a curve over its foot pad. Generally going to be smaller than grizzly bear paw.

Grizzly Bear

FRONT REAR

Has long claws that extend out further from their toes. Its toes also are held closer together, forming almost a straight line above the foot pad.

Rodent

Beaver

FRONT   REAR

Webbed hind feet with 5 toes (4.5-7"). Sometime 4-toed prints.

Porcupine

FRONT   REAR

Usually only see pads in prints (1-2"). Pigeon-toed.

Muskrat

FRONT   REAR

Hand-like like raccoon but smaller (2.3").

Mouse

FRONT   REAR

Larger back feet (1.5 - 2"), smaller front feet (0.25-0.5").

Squirrel

FRONT   REAR

Larger back feet (1.5-2"), smaller front feet (1-1.5").

Hoof

Mountain Goat

FRONT   REAR

Have toes that spread when they step, creating a distinctive V shape at the top of their print.

Bighorn Sheep

FRONT   REAR

Similar to deer but with straighter edges and less pointed. More blocky and less shaped like a heart.

Wild Hog

FRONT   REAR

Often confused with deer but toes are wider, rounder and blunter and don't come to a point. Have dew claw that rests slightly outside print.

Reptile / Amphibian

Alligator

FRONT

REAR

Large feet with four toes on front prints and five toes on rear prints. Front are wide in heel, rear are longer, narrow and pointed heel.

Lizard

FRONT   REAR

Lightweight and don't leave much of a track. Might leave small scuff from feet and small tail drag.

Frog

FRONT   REAR

Have four bulbous toes in front and five in hind prints. Front toes point slightly inward producing a "K" shaped print, while rear toes slope upward and outward.

Other Common

Raccoon

FRONT

REAR

Five toes resembles hand of a baby. Front print smaller (1-3") with C-shaped heel pad. Rear print longer (1.5-4") heel pad.

Opossum

FRONT   REAR

Five fingers and human hand shape. Opposable thumbs on hind feet .

Rabbit
REAR

FRONT

Larger hind feet, smaller front feet. Hoppers producing a "Y" shaped track.

Skunk

FRONT

REAR

Five toes on their hind and front feet. Front and rear are approximately same size. Claws show up in many prints.

Otter

FRONT   REAR

Five toes and short claws give their prints a pointed look. Toes are partially webbed.

Armadillo
REAR

FRONT

Four long toe prints with sharp claw at tip. Front print show distinct 'V' between middle toes.

Sketch

Sketch / Notes

General

Date: _____ Location: _____

Environment: ◯ Mud ◯ Snow ◯ Soft Garden Soil ◯ Sand

Time of Day: ◯ Morning ◯ Midday ◯ Evening ◯ Time_____

Front Toes: ◯ Five ◯ Four ◯ Three ◯ Two

Rear Toes: ◯ Five ◯ Four ◯ Three ◯ Two

Track Symmetry: ◯ Symmetric ◯ Asymmetric

Claws / Nails: ◯ Visible ◯ Not Visible   Webbing: ◯ Yes ◯ No

Surroundings: _____

Movement Pattern: ◯ Zig-Zaggler ◯ Trot ◯ Lope ◯ Gallop

Notes: _____

Canine

Wolf

FRONT REAR

Biggest in this group with a long (4") and wide print.

Coyote

FRONT REAR

Slightly smaller than wolves with print more narrow (2.5 to 3.5").

Fox

FRONT REAR

Smallest in the group with print (2 to 3") and fuzzy around edges.

Dog

FRONT REAR

Similar to wolf/coyote with thicker nails.

Feline

Cougar / Mountain Lion

FRONT REAR

Largest in the group (greater than 3"). Size of domestic dog.

Lynx

FRONT REAR

Same as cougar but smaller in size and not as defined due to fur around paws.

Bobcat

FRONT REAR

Smaller tracks (2"). Often confused with coyote or fox but lacks nails. Round shape.

House Cat

FRONT REAR

Small (1 to 1.5"). Similar to domestic dog, meander when walking.

Bird

Crow

Standard bird track: 3 forward, 1 rear. Print 2-2.5".

Grouse

Small ground birds with only 3 forward toes. Print 2" long.

Turkey

Similar to grouse but much larger prints (4") long.

Duck

Webbing gives its print distinctive shape.

Bear

Black Bear

FRONT REAR

Has short claws and its toes spread out in a curve over its foot pad. Generally going to be smaller than grizzly bear paw.

Grizzly Bear
FRONT REAR

Has long claws that extend out further from their toes. Its toes also are held closer together, forming almost a straight line above the foot pad.

Rodent

Beaver

FRONT   REAR
Webbed hind feet with 5 toes (4.5-7"). Sometime 4-toed prints.

Porcupine

FRONT   REAR
Usually only see pads in prints (1-2"). Pigeon-toed.

Muskrat

FRONT   REAR
Hand-like like raccoon but smaller (2.3").

Mouse

FRONT   REAR
Larger back feet (1.5 - 2"), smaller front feet (0.25-0.5").

Squirrel
FRONT   REAR
Larger back feet (1.5-2"), smaller front feet (1-1.5").

Hoof

Mountain Goat

FRONT   REAR
Have toes that spread when they step, creating a distinctive V shape at the top of their print.

Bighorn Sheep
FRONT   REAR
Similar to deer but with straighter edges and less pointed. More blocky and less shaped like a heart.

Wild Hog

FRONT   REAR
Often confused with deer but toes are wider, rounder and blunter and don't come to a point. Have dew claw that rests slightly outside print.

Reptile / Amphibian

Alligator

FRONT
REAR
Large feet with four toes on front prints and five toes on rear prints. Front are wide in heel, rear are longer, narrow and pointed heel.

Lizard

FRONT   REAR
Lightweight and don't leave much of a track. Might leave small scuff from feet and small tail drag.

Frog
FRONT   REAR
Have four bulbous toes in front and five in hind prints. Front toes point slightly inward producing a "K" shaped print, while rear toes slope upward and outward.

Other Common

Raccoon

FRONT
REAR
Five toes resembles hand of a baby. Front print smaller (1-3") with C-shaped heel pad. Rear print longer (1.5-4") heel pad.

Opossum
FRONT   REAR
Five fingers and human hand shape. Opposable thumbs on hind feet.

Rabbit
REAR
FRONT
Larger hind feet, smaller front feet. Hoppers producing a "Y" shaped track.

Skunk

FRONT
REAR
Five toes on their hind and front feet. Front and rear are approximately same size. Claws show up in many prints.

Otter

FRONT   REAR
Five toes and short claws give their prints a pointed look. Toes are partially webbed.

Armadillo
REAR
FRONT
Four long toe prints with sharp claw at tip. Front print show distinct "V" between middle toes.

Sketch

Sketch / Notes

General

Date: _____   Location: _____

Environment: ◯ Mud   ◯ Snow   ◯ Soft Garden Soil   ◯ Sand

Time of Day: ◯ Morning   ◯ Midday   ◯ Evening   ◯ Time_____

Front Toes: ◯ Five   ◯ Four   ◯ Three   ◯ Two

Rear Toes: ◯ Five   ◯ Four   ◯ Three   ◯ Two

Track Symmetry: ◯ Symmetric   ◯ Asymmetric

Claws / Nails: ◯ Visible   ◯ Not Visible   Webbing: ◯ Yes   ◯ No

Surroundings: _____

Movement Pattern: ◯ Zig-Zaggler   ◯ Trot   ◯ Lope   ◯ Gallop

Notes: _____

Canine

Wolf	Coyote	Fox	Dog
FRONT REAR	FRONT REAR	FRONT REAR	FRONT REAR
Biggest in this group with a long (4") and wide print.	Slightly smaller than wolves with print more narrow (2.5 to 3.5").	Smallest in the group with print (2 to 3") and fuzzy around edges.	Similar to wolf/coyote with thicker nails.

Feline

Cougar / Mountain Lion	Lynx	Bobcat	House Cat
FRONT REAR	FRONT REAR	FRONT REAR	FRONT REAR
Largest in the group (greater than 3"). Size of domestic dog.	Same as cougar but smaller in size and not as defined due to fur around paws.	Smaller tracks (2"). Often confused with coyote or fox but lacks nails. Round shape.	Small (1 to 1.5"). Similar to domestic dog, meander when walking.

Bird

Crow	Grouse	Turkey	Duck
Standard bird track: 3 forward, 1 rear. Print 2-2.5".	Small ground birds with only 3 forward toes. Print 2" long.	Similar to grouse but much larger prints (4") long.	Webbing gives its print distinctive shape.

Bear

Black Bear

FRONT   REAR

Has short claws and its toes spread out in a curve over its foot pad Generally going to be smaller than grizzly bear paw.

Grizzly Bear
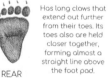
FRONT   REAR

Has long claws that extend out further from their toes. Its toes also are held closer together, forming almost a straight line above the foot pad.

Rodent

Beaver

FRONT   REAR
Webbed hind feet with 5 toes (4.5-7"). Sometime 4-toed prints.

Porcupine

FRONT   REAR
Usually only see pads in prints (1-2"). Pigeon-toed.

Muskrat

FRONT   REAR
Hand-like like raccoon but smaller (2.3").

Mouse

FRONT   REAR
Larger back feet (1.5 - 2"), smaller front feet (0.25-0.5").

Squirrel

FRONT   REAR
Larger back feet (1.5-2"), smaller front feet (1-1.5").

Hoof

Mountain Goat

FRONT   REAR
Have toes that spread when they step, creating a distinctive V shape at the top of their print.

Bighorn Sheep

FRONT   REAR
Similar to deer but with straighter edges and less pointed. More blocky and less shaped like a heart.

Wild Hog

FRONT   REAR
Often confused with deer but toes are wider, rounder and blunter and don't come to a point. Have dew claw that rests slightly outside print.

Reptile / Amphibian

Alligator

FRONT
REAR
Large feet with four toes on front prints and five toes on rear prints. Front are wide in heel, rear are longer, narrow and pointed heel.

Lizard

FRONT   REAR
Lightweight and don't leave much of a track. Might leave small scuff from feet and small tail drag.

Frog

FRONT   REAR
Have four bulbous toes in front and five in hind prints. Front toes point slightly inward producing a "K" shaped print, while rear toes slope upward and outward.

Other Common

Raccoon

FRONT
REAR
Five toes resembles hand of a baby. Front print smaller (1-3") with C-shaped heel pad. Rear print longer (1.5-4") heel pad.

Opossum

FRONT   REAR
Five fingers and human hand shape. Opposable thumbs on hind feet.

Rabbit

REAR
FRONT
Larger hind feet, smaller front feet. Hoppers producing a "Y" shaped track.

Skunk

FRONT
REAR
Five toes on their hind and front feet. Front and rear are approximately same size. Claws show up in many prints.

Otter
FRONT   REAR
Five toes and short claws give their prints a pointed look. Toes are partially webbed.

Armadillo
REAR
FRONT
Four long toe prints with sharp claw at tip. Front print show distinct "V" between middle toes.

Sketch / Notes

Sketch

General

Date: _____ Location: _____

Environment: ⬭ Mud ⬭ Snow ⬭ Soft Garden Soil ⬭ Sand

Time of Day: ⬭ Morning ⬭ Midday ⬭ Evening ⬭ Time _____

Front Toes: ⬭ Five ⬭ Four ⬭ Three ⬭ Two

Rear Toes: ⬭ Five ⬭ Four ⬭ Three ⬭ Two

Track Symmetry: ⬭ Symmetric ⬭ Asymmetric

Claws / Nails: ⬭ Visible ⬭ Not Visible   Webbing: ⬭ Yes ⬭ No

Surroundings: _____

Movement Pattern: ⬭ Zig-Zaggler ⬭ Trot ⬭ Lope ⬭ Gallop

Notes: _____

Canine

Wolf	Coyote	Fox	Dog

FRONT   REAR   FRONT   REAR   FRONT   REAR   FRONT   REAR

Biggest in this group with a long (4") and wide print. | Slightly smaller than wolves with print more narrow (2.5 to 3.5"). | Smallest in the group with print (2 to 3") and fuzzy around edges. | Similar to wolf/coyote with thicker nails.

Feline

Cougar / Mountain Lion	Lynx	Bobcat	House Cat

FRONT   REAR   FRONT   REAR   FRONT   REAR   FRONT   REAR

Largest in the group (greater than 3"). Size of domestic dog. | Same as cougar but smaller in size and not as defined due to fur around paws. | Smaller tracks (2"). Often confused with coyote or fox but lacks nails. Round shape. | Small (1 to 1.5"). Similar to domestic dog, meander when walking.

Bird

Crow	Grouse	Turkey	Duck

Standard bird track: 3 forward, 1 rear. Print 2-2.5". | Small ground birds with only 3 forward toes. Print 2" long. | Similar to grouse but much larger prints (4") long. | Webbing gives its print distinctive shape.

Bear

Black Bear

FRONT   REAR

Has short claws and its toes spread out in a curve over its foot pad. Generally going to be smaller than grizzly bear paw.

Grizzly Bear

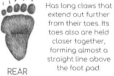

FRONT   REAR

Has long claws that extend out further from their toes. Its toes also are held closer together, forming almost a straight line above the foot pad.

Rodent

Beaver

FRONT   REAR
Webbed hind feet with 5 toes (4.5-7"). Sometime 4-toed prints.

Porcupine

FRONT   REAR
Usually only see pads in prints (1-2"). Pigeon-toed.

Muskrat
FRONT   REAR
Hand-like like raccoon but smaller (2.3").

Mouse

FRONT   REAR
Larger back feet (1.5 - 2"), smaller front feet (0.25-0.5").

Squirrel

FRONT   REAR
Larger back feet (1.5-2"), smaller front feet (1-1.5").

Hoof

Mountain Goat

FRONT   REAR
Have toes that spread when they step, creating a distinctive V shape at the top of their print.

Bighorn Sheep

FRONT   REAR
Similar to deer but with straighter edges and less pointed. More blocky and less shaped like a heart.

Wild Hog

FRONT   REAR
Often confused with deer but toes are wider, rounder and blunter and don't come to a point. Have dew claw that rests slightly outside print.

Reptile / Amphibian

Alligator

FRONT
REAR
Large feet with four toes on front prints and five toes on rear prints. Front are wide in heel, rear are longer, narrow and pointed heel.

Lizard

FRONT   REAR
Lightweight and don't leave much of a track. Might leave small scuff from feet and small tail drag.

Frog

FRONT   REAR
Have four bulbous toes in front and five in hind prints. Front toes point slightly inward producing a "K" shaped print, while rear toes slope upward and outward.

Other Common

Raccoon

FRONT
REAR
Five toes resembles hand of a baby. Front print smaller (1-3") with C-shaped heel pad. Rear print longer (1.5-4") heel pad.

Opossum

FRONT   REAR
Five fingers and human hand shape. Opposable thumbs on hind feet.

Rabbit
REAR

FRONT
Larger hind feet, smaller front feet. Hoppers producing a "Y" shaped track.

Skunk

FRONT
REAR
Five toes on their hind and front feet. Front and rear are approximately same size. Claws show up in many prints.

Otter

FRONT   REAR
Five toes and short claws give their prints a pointed look. Toes are partially webbed.

Armadillo
REAR

FRONT
Four long toe prints with sharp claw at tip. Front print show distinct "V" between middle toes.

Sketch / Notes

Sketch

_____
_____
_____
_____
_____
_____
_____
_____
_____
_____

General

Date: _____ Location: _____

Environment: ◯ Mud ◯ Snow ◯ Soft Garden Soil ◯ Sand

Time of Day: ◯ Morning ◯ Midday ◯ Evening ◯ Time _____

Front Toes: ◯ Five ◯ Four ◯ Three ◯ Two

Rear Toes: ◯ Five ◯ Four ◯ Three ◯ Two

Track Symmetry: ◯ Symmetric ◯ Asymmetric

Claws / Nails: ◯ Visible ◯ Not Visible   Webbing: ◯ Yes ◯ No

Surroundings: _____

Movement Pattern: ◯ Zig-Zaggler ◯ Trot ◯ Lope ◯ Gallop

Notes: _____

Canine

Wolf

FRONT   REAR

Biggest in this group with a long (4") and wide print.

Coyote
FRONT   REAR

Slightly smaller than wolves with print more narrow (2.5 to 3.5").

Fox
FRONT   REAR

Smallest in the group with print (2 to 3") and fuzzy around edges.

Dog
FRONT   REAR

Similar to wolf/coyote with thicker nails.

Feline

Cougar / Mountain Lion
FRONT   REAR

Largest in the group (greater than 3"). Size of domestic dog.

Lynx
FRONT   REAR

Same as cougar but smaller in size and not as defined due to fur around paws.

Bobcat
FRONT   REAR

Smaller tracks (2"). Often confused with coyote or fox but lacks nails. Round shape.

House Cat
FRONT   REAR

Small (1 to 1.5"). Similar to domestic dog, meander when walking.

Bird

Crow

Standard bird track: 3 forward, 1 rear. Print 2-2.5".

Grouse

Small ground birds with only 3 forward toes. Print 2" long.

Turkey

Similar to grouse but much larger prints (4") long.

Duck

Webbing gives its print distinctive shape.

Bear

Black Bear
FRONT   REAR

Has short claws and its toes spread out in a curve over its foot pad. Generally going to be smaller than grizzly bear paw.

Grizzly Bear
FRONT   REAR

Has long claws that extend out further from their toes. Its toes also are held closer together, forming almost a straight line above the foot pad.

Rodent

Beaver

FRONT REAR
Webbed hind feet with 5 toes (4.5-7"). Sometime 4-toed prints.

Porcupine

FRONT REAR
Usually only see pads in prints (1-2"). Pigeon-toed.

Muskrat

FRONT REAR
Hand-like like raccoon but smaller (2.3").

Mouse
FRONT REAR
Larger back feet (1.5 - 2"), smaller front feet (0.25-0.5").

Squirrel

FRONT REAR
Larger back feet (1.5-2"), smaller front feet (1-1.5").

Hoof

Mountain Goat

FRONT REAR
Have toes that spread when they step, creating a distinctive V shape at the top of their print.

Bighorn Sheep

FRONT REAR
Similar to deer but with straighter edges and less pointed. More blocky and less shaped like a heart.

Wild Hog

FRONT REAR
Often confused with deer but toes are wider, rounder and blunter and don't come to a point. Have dew claw that rests slightly outside print.

Reptile / Amphibian

Alligator

FRONT
REAR
Large feet with four toes on front prints and five toes on rear prints. Front are wide in heel, rear are longer, narrow and pointed heel.

Lizard

FRONT REAR
Lightweight and don't leave much of a track. Might leave small scuff from feet and small tail drag.

Frog

FRONT REAR
Have four bulbous toes in front and five in hind prints. Front toes point slightly inward producing a "K" shaped print, while rear toes slope upward and outward.

Other Common

Raccoon

FRONT
REAR
Five toes resembles hand of a baby. Front print smaller (1-3") with C-shaped heel pad. Rear print longer (1.5-4") heel pad.

Opossum

FRONT REAR
Five fingers and human hand shape. Opposable thumbs on hind feet .

Rabbit

REAR
FRONT
Larger hind feet, smaller front feet. Hoppers producing a "Y" shaped track.

Skunk

FRONT
REAR
Five toes on their hind and front feet. Front and rear are approximately same size. Claws show up in many prints.

Otter

FRONT REAR
Five toes and short claws give their prints a pointed look. Toes are partially webbed.

Armadillo

REAR
FRONT
Four long toe prints with sharp claw at tip. Front print show distinct "V" between middle toes.

Sketch

Sketch / Notes

General

Date: _____ Location: _____

Environment: ○ Mud ○ Snow ○ Soft Garden Soil ○ Sand

Time of Day: ○ Morning ○ Midday ○ Evening ○ Time _____

Front Toes: ○ Five ○ Four ○ Three ○ Two

Rear Toes: ○ Five ○ Four ○ Three ○ Two

Track Symmetry: ○ Symmetric ○ Asymmetric

Claws / Nails: ○ Visible ○ Not Visible   Webbing: ○ Yes ○ No

Surroundings: _____

Movement Pattern: ○ Zig-Zaggler ○ Trot ○ Lope ○ Gallop

Notes: _____

Canine

Wolf	Coyote	Fox	Dog
FRONT REAR	FRONT REAR	FRONT REAR	FRONT REAR
Biggest in this group with a long (4") and wide print.	Slightly smaller than wolves with print more narrow (2.5 to 3.5").	Smallest in the group with print (2 to 3") and fuzzy around edges.	Similar to wolf/coyote with thicker nails.

Feline

Cougar / Mountain Lion	Lynx	Bobcat	House Cat
FRONT REAR	FRONT REAR	FRONT REAR	FRONT REAR
Largest in the group (greater than 3"). Size of domestic dog.	Same as cougar but smaller in size and not as defined due to fur around paws.	Smaller tracks (2"). Often confused with coyote or fox but lacks nails. Round shape.	Small (1 to 1.5"). Similar to domestic dog, meander when walking.

Bird

Crow	Grouse	Turkey	Duck
Standard bird track: 3 forward, 1 rear. Print 2-2.5".	Small ground birds with only 3 forward toes. Print 2" long.	Similar to grouse but much larger prints (4") long.	Webbing gives its print distinctive shape.

Bear

Black Bear

FRONT REAR

Has short claws and its toes spread out in a curve over its foot pad. Generally going to be smaller than grizzly bear paw.

Grizzly Bear

FRONT REAR

Has long claws that extend out further from their toes. Its toes also are held closer together, forming almost a straight line above the foot pad.

Rodent

Beaver

FRONT   REAR

Webbed hind feet with 5 toes (4.5-7"). Sometime 4-toed prints.

Porcupine

FRONT   REAR

Usually only see pads in prints (1-2"). Pigeon-toed.

Muskrat

FRONT   REAR

Hand-like like raccoon but smaller (2.3").

Mouse

FRONT   REAR

Larger back feet (1.5 - 2"), smaller front feet (0.25-0.5").

Squirrel
FRONT   REAR

Larger back feet (1.5-2"), smaller front feet (1-1.5").

Hoof

Mountain Goat

FRONT   REAR

Have toes that spread when they step, creating a distinctive V shape at the top of their print.

Bighorn Sheep

FRONT   REAR

Similar to deer but with straighter edges and less pointed. More blocky and less shaped like a heart.

Wild Hog

FRONT   REAR

Often confused with deer but toes are wider, rounder and blunter and don't come to a point. Have dew claw that rests slightly outside print.

Reptile / Amphibian

Alligator

FRONT
REAR

Large feet with four toes on front prints and five toes on rear prints. Front are wide in heel, rear are longer, narrow and pointed heel.

Lizard

FRONT   REAR

Lightweight and don't leave much of a track. Might leave small scuff from feet and small tail drag.

Frog

FRONT   REAR

Have four bulbous toes in front and five in hind prints. Front toes point slightly inward producing a "K" shaped print, while rear toes slope upward and outward.

Other Common

Raccoon

FRONT
REAR

Five toes resembles hand of a baby. Front print smaller (1-3") with C-shaped heel pad. Rear print longer (1.5-4") heel pad.

Opossum

FRONT   REAR

Five fingers and human hand shape. Opposable thumbs on hind feet.

Rabbit
REAR

FRONT

Larger hind feet, smaller front feet. Hoppers producing a "Y" shaped track.

Skunk

FRONT
REAR

Five toes on their hind and front feet. Front and rear are approximately same size. Claws show up in many prints.

Otter

FRONT   REAR

Five toes and short claws give their prints a pointed look. Toes are partially webbed.

Armadillo
REAR

FRONT

Four long toe prints with sharp claw at tip. Front print show distinct "V" between middle toes.

Sketch

Sketch / Notes

_____
_____
_____
_____
_____
_____
_____
_____
_____
_____
_____

General

Date: _____ Location: _____

Environment: ◯ Mud ◯ Snow ◯ Soft Garden Soil ◯ Sand

Time of Day: ◯ Morning ◯ Midday ◯ Evening ◯ Time_____

Front Toes: ◯ Five ◯ Four ◯ Three ◯ Two

Rear Toes: ◯ Five ◯ Four ◯ Three ◯ Two

Track Symmetry: ◯ Symmetric ◯ Asymmetric

Claws / Nails: ◯ Visible ◯ Not Visible   Webbing: ◯ Yes ◯ No

Surroundings: _____

Movement Pattern: ◯ Zig-Zaggler   ◯ Trot   ◯ Lope   ◯ Gallop

Notes: _____

Canine

Wolf

FRONT   REAR

Biggest in this group with a long (4") and wide print.

Coyote
FRONT   REAR

Slightly smaller than wolves with print more narrow (2.5 to 3.5").

Fox
FRONT   REAR

Smallest in the group with print (2 to 3") and fuzzy around edges.

Dog
FRONT   REAR

Similar to wolf/coyote with thicker nails.

Feline

Cougar / Mountain Lion
FRONT   REAR

Largest in the group (greater than 3"). Size of domestic dog.

Lynx
FRONT   REAR

Same as cougar but smaller in size and not as defined due to fur around paws.

Bobcat
FRONT   REAR

Smaller tracks (2"). Often confused with coyote or fox but lacks nails. Round shape.

House Cat
FRONT   REAR

Small (1 to 1.5"). Similar to domestic dog, meander when walking.

Bird

Crow

Standard bird track: 3 forward, 1 rear. Print 2-2.5".

Grouse

Small ground birds with only 3 forward toes. Print 2" long.

Turkey

Similar to grouse but much larger prints (4") long.

Duck

Webbing gives its print distinctive shape.

Bear

Black Bear

FRONT   REAR

Has short claws and its toes spread out in a curve over its foot pad. Generally going to be smaller than grizzly bear paw.

Grizzly Bear

FRONT   REAR

Has long claws that extend out further from their toes. Its toes also are held closer together, forming almost a straight line above the foot pad.

Rodent

Beaver

FRONT   REAR
Webbed hind feet with 5 toes (4.5-7"). Sometime 4-toed prints.

Porcupine
FRONT REAR
Usually only see pads in prints (1-2"). Pigeon-toed.

Muskrat

FRONT REAR
Hand-like like raccoon but smaller (2.3").

Mouse
FRONT REAR
Larger back feet (1.5 - 2"), smaller front feet (0.25-0.5").

Squirrel

FRONT   REAR
Larger back feet (1.5-2"), smaller front feet (1-1.5").

Hoof

Mountain Goat

FRONT   REAR
Have toes that spread when they step, creating a distinctive V shape at the top of their print.

Bighorn Sheep

FRONT   REAR
Similar to deer but with straighter edges and less pointed. More blocky and less shaped like a heart.

Wild Hog

FRONT   REAR
Often confused with deer but toes are wider, rounder and blunter and don't come to a point. Have dew claw that rests slightly outside print.

Reptile / Amphibian

Alligator

FRONT   REAR
Large feet with four toes on front prints and five toes on rear prints. Front are wide in heel, rear are longer, narrow and pointed heel.

Lizard

FRONT REAR
Lightweight and don't leave much of a track. Might leave small scuff from feet and small tail drag.

Frog

FRONT   REAR
Have four bulbous toes in front and five in hind prints. Front toes point slightly inward producing a "K" shaped print, while rear toes slope upward and outward.

Other Common

Raccoon

FRONT   REAR
Five toes resembles hand of a baby. Front print smaller (1-3") with C-shaped heel pad. Rear print longer (1.5-4") heel pad.

Opossum

FRONT   REAR
Five fingers and human hand shape. Opposable thumbs on hind feet .

Rabbit
REAR

FRONT
Larger hind feet, smaller front feet. Hoppers producing a "Y" shaped track.

Skunk

FRONT   REAR
Five toes on their hind and front feet. Front and rear are approximately same size. Claws show up in many prints.

Otter

FRONT REAR
Five toes and short claws give their prints a pointed look. Toes are partially webbed.

Armadillo
REAR

FRONT
Four long toe prints with sharp claw at tip. Front print show distinct "V" between middle toes.

Sketch

Sketch / Notes

General

Date: _____ Location: _____

Environment: ⬭ Mud ⬭ Snow ⬭ Soft Garden Soil ⬭ Sand

Time of Day: ⬭ Morning ⬭ Midday ⬭ Evening ⬭ Time _____

Front Toes: ⬭ Five ⬭ Four ⬭ Three ⬭ Two

Rear Toes: ⬭ Five ⬭ Four ⬭ Three ⬭ Two

Track Symmetry: ⬭ Symmetric ⬭ Asymmetric

Claws / Nails: ⬭ Visible ⬭ Not Visible   Webbing: ⬭ Yes ⬭ No

Surroundings: _____

Movement Pattern: ⬭ Zig-Zaggler ⬭ Trot ⬭ Lope ⬭ Gallop

Notes: _____

Canine

Wolf

FRONT   REAR

Biggest in this group with a long (4") and wide print.

Coyote

FRONT   REAR

Slightly smaller than wolves with print more narrow (2.5 to 3.5").

Fox

FRONT   REAR

Smallest in the group with print (2 to 3") and fuzzy around edges.

Dog

FRONT   REAR

Similar to wolf/coyote with thicker nails.

Feline

Cougar / Mountain Lion

FRONT   REAR

Largest in the group (greater than 3"). Size of domestic dog.

Lynx

FRONT   REAR

Same as cougar but smaller in size and not as defined due to fur around paws.

Bobcat

FRONT   REAR

Smaller tracks (2"). Often confused with coyote or fox but lacks nails. Round shape.

House Cat

FRONT   REAR

Small (1 to 1.5"). Similar to domestic dog, meander when walking.

Bird

Crow

Standard bird track: 3 forward, 1 rear. Print 2-2.5".

Grouse

Small ground birds with only 3 forward toes. Print 2" long.

Turkey

Similar to grouse but much larger prints (4") long.

Duck

Webbing gives its print distinctive shape.

Bear

Black Bear

FRONT   REAR

Has short claws and its toes spread out in a curve over its foot pad. Generally going to be smaller than grizzly bear paw.

Grizzly Bear

FRONT   REAR

Has long claws that extend out further from their toes. Its toes also are held closer together, forming almost a straight line above the foot pad.

Rodent

Beaver

FRONT REAR
Webbed hind feet with 5 toes (4.5-7"). Sometime 4-toed prints.

Porcupine
FRONT REAR
Usually only see pads in prints (1-2"). Pigeon-toed.

Muskrat
FRONT REAR
Hand-like like raccoon but smaller (2.3").

Mouse

FRONT REAR
Larger back feet (1.5 - 2"), smaller front feet (0.25-0.5").

Squirrel

FRONT REAR
Larger back feet (1.5-2"), smaller front feet (1-1.5").

Hoof

Mountain Goat

FRONT REAR
Have toes that spread when they step, creating a distinctive V shape at the top of their print.

Bighorn Sheep

FRONT REAR
Similar to deer but with straighter edges and less pointed. More blocky and less shaped like a heart.

Wild Hog

FRONT REAR
Often confused with deer but toes are wider, rounder and blunter and don't come to a point. Have dew claw that rests slightly outside print.

Reptile / Amphibian

Alligator

FRONT REAR
Large feet with four toes on front prints and five toes on rear prints. Front are wide in heel, rear are longer, narrow and pointed heel.

Lizard

FRONT REAR
Lightweight and don't leave much of a track. Might leave small scuff from feet and small tail drag.

Frog

FRONT REAR
Have four bulbous toes in front and five in hind prints. Front toes point slightly inward producing a "K" shaped print, while rear toes slope upward and outward.

Other Common

Raccoon

FRONT REAR
Five toes resembles hand of a baby. Front print smaller (1-3") with C-shaped heel pad. Rear print longer (1.5-4") heel pad.

Opossum

FRONT REAR
Five fingers and human hand shape. Opposable thumbs on hind feet.

Rabbit
REAR
FRONT

Larger hind feet, smaller front feet. Hoppers producing a "Y" shaped track.

Skunk

FRONT REAR
Five toes on their hind and front feet. Front and rear are approximately same size. Claws show up in many prints.

Otter

FRONT REAR
Five toes and short claws give their prints a pointed look. Toes are partially webbed.

Armadillo
REAR

FRONT
Four long toe prints with sharp claw at tip. Front print show distinct "V" between middle toes.

Sketch

Sketch / Notes

General

Date: _____   Location: _____

Environment: ◯ Mud   ◯ Snow   ◯ Soft Garden Soil   ◯ Sand

Time of Day: ◯ Morning   ◯ Midday   ◯ Evening   ◯ Time _____

Front Toes: ◯ Five   ◯ Four   ◯ Three   ◯ Two

Rear Toes: ◯ Five   ◯ Four   ◯ Three   ◯ Two

Track Symmetry: ◯ Symmetric   ◯ Asymmetric

Claws / Nails: ◯ Visible   ◯ Not Visible   Webbing: ◯ Yes   ◯ No

Surroundings: _____

Movement Pattern: ◯ Zig-Zaggler   ◯ Trot   ◯ Lope   ◯ Gallop

Notes: _____

Canine

Wolf

FRONT   REAR

Biggest in this group with a long (4") and wide print.

Coyote

FRONT   REAR

Slightly smaller than wolves with print more narrow (2.5 to 3.5").

Fox
FRONT   REAR

Smallest in the group with print (2 to 3") and fuzzy around edges.

Dog
FRONT   REAR

Similar to wolf/coyote with thicker nails.

Feline

Cougar / Mountain Lion

FRONT   REAR

Largest in the group (greater than 3"). Size of domestic dog.

Lynx
FRONT   REAR

Same as cougar but smaller in size and not as defined due to fur around paws.

Bobcat

FRONT   REAR

Smaller tracks (2"). Often confused with coyote or fox but lacks nails. Round shape.

House Cat

FRONT   REAR

Small (1 to 1.5"). Similar to domestic dog, meander when walking.

Bird

Crow

Standard bird track: 3 forward, 1 rear. Print 2-2.5".

Grouse

Small ground birds with only 3 forward toes. Print 2" long.

Turkey

Similar to grouse but much larger prints (4") long.

Duck

Webbing gives its print distinctive shape.

Bear

Black Bear

FRONT   REAR

Has short claws and its toes spread out in a curve over its foot pad. Generally going to be smaller than grizzly bear paw.

Grizzly Bear

FRONT   REAR

Has long claws that extend out further from their toes. Its toes also are held closer together, forming almost a straight line above the foot pad.

Rodent

Beaver

FRONT REAR
Webbed hind feet with 5 toes (4.5-7"). Sometime 4-toed prints.

Porcupine

FRONT REAR
Usually only see pads in prints (1-2"). Pigeon-toed.

Muskrat

FRONT REAR
Hand-like like raccoon but smaller (2.3").

Mouse

FRONT REAR
Larger back feet (1.5 - 2"), smaller front feet (0.25-0.5").

Squirrel

FRONT REAR
Larger back feet (1.5-2"), smaller front feet (1-1.5").

Hoof

Mountain Goat

FRONT REAR
Have toes that spread when they step, creating a distinctive V shape at the top of their print.

Bighorn Sheep

FRONT REAR
Similar to deer but with straighter edges and less pointed. More blocky and less shaped like a heart.

Wild Hog

FRONT REAR
Often confused with deer but toes are wider, rounder and blunter and don't come to a point. Have dew claw that rests slightly outside print.

Reptile / Amphibian

Alligator

FRONT
REAR
Large feet with four toes on front prints and five toes on rear prints. Front are wide in heel, rear are longer, narrow and pointed heel.

Lizard

FRONT REAR
Lightweight and don't leave much of a track. Might leave small scuff from feet and small tail drag.

Frog

FRONT REAR
Have four bulbous toes in front and five in hind prints. Front toes point slightly inward producing a "K" shaped print, while rear toes slope upward and outward.

Other Common

Raccoon

FRONT
REAR
Five toes resembles hand of a baby. Front print smaller (1-3") with C-shaped heel pad. Rear print longer (1.5-4") heel pad.

Opossum

FRONT REAR
Five fingers and human hand shape. Opposable thumbs on hind feet.

Rabbit
REAR

FRONT
Larger hind feet, smaller front feet. Hoppers producing a "Y" shaped track.

Skunk

FRONT
REAR
Five toes on their hind and front feet. Front and rear are approximately same size. Claws show up in many prints.

Otter

FRONT REAR
Five toes and short claws give their prints a pointed look. Toes are partially webbed.

Armadillo
REAR

FRONT
Four long toe prints with sharp claw at tip. Front print show distinct "V" between middle toes.

Sketch

Sketch / Notes

_____
_____
_____
_____
_____
_____
_____
_____
_____
_____
_____

General

Date: _____ Location: _____

Environment: ◯ Mud ◯ Snow ◯ Soft Garden Soil ◯ Sand

Time of Day: ◯ Morning ◯ Midday ◯ Evening ◯ Time _____

Front Toes: ◯ Five ◯ Four ◯ Three ◯ Two

Rear Toes: ◯ Five ◯ Four ◯ Three ◯ Two

Track Symmetry: ◯ Symmetric ◯ Asymmetric

Claws / Nails: ◯ Visible ◯ Not Visible   Webbing: ◯ Yes ◯ No

Surroundings: _____

Movement Pattern: ◯ Zig-Zaggler ◯ Trot ◯ Lope ◯ Gallop

Notes: _____

Canine

Wolf

FRONT   REAR

Biggest in this group with a long (4") and wide print.

Coyote
FRONT   REAR

Slightly smaller than wolves with print more narrow (2.5 to 3.5").

Fox
FRONT   REAR

Smallest in the group with print (2 to 3") and fuzzy around edges.

Dog
FRONT   REAR

Similar to wolf/coyote with thicker nails.

Feline

Cougar / Mountain Lion

FRONT   REAR

Largest in the group (greater than 3"). Size of domestic dog.

Lynx
FRONT   REAR

Same as cougar but smaller in size and not as defined due to fur around paws.

Bobcat
FRONT   REAR

Smaller tracks (2"). Often confused with coyote or fox but lacks nails. Round shape.

House Cat
FRONT   REAR

Small (1 to 1.5"). Similar to domestic dog, meander when walking.

Bird

Crow

Standard bird track: 3 forward, 1 rear. Print 2-2.5".

Grouse

Small ground birds with only 3 forward toes. Print 2" long.

Turkey

Similar to grouse but much larger prints (4") long.

Duck

Webbing gives its print distinctive shape.

Bear

Black Bear

FRONT   REAR

Has short claws and its toes spread out in a curve over its foot pad. Generally going to be smaller than grizzly bear paw.

Grizzly Bear

FRONT   REAR

Has long claws that extend out further from their toes. Its toes also are held closer together, forming almost a straight line above the foot pad.

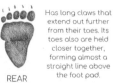

Beaver

FRONT   REAR

Webbed hind feet with 5 toes (4.5-7"). Sometime 4-toed prints.

Porcupine

FRONT REAR

Usually only see pads in prints (1-2"). Pigeon-toed.

Muskrat

FRONT   REAR

Hand-like like raccoon but smaller (2.3").

Mouse

FRONT REAR

Larger back feet (1.5 - 2"), smaller front feet (0.25-0.5").

Squirrel

FRONT   REAR

Larger back feet (1.5-2"), smaller front feet (1-1.5").

Mountain Goat

FRONT   REAR

Have toes that spread when they step, creating a distinctive V shape at the top of their print.

Bighorn Sheep

FRONT   REAR

Similar to deer but with straighter edges and less pointed. More blocky and less shaped like a heart.

Wild Hog

FRONT   REAR

Often confused with deer but toes are wider, rounder and blunter and don't come to a point. Have dew claw that rests slightly outside print.

Alligator

FRONT

REAR

Large feet with four toes on front prints and five toes on rear prints. Front are wide in heel, rear are longer, narrow and pointed heel.

Lizard

FRONT   REAR

Lightweight and don't leave much of a track. Might leave small scuff from feet and small tail drag.

Frog

FRONT   REAR

Have four bulbous toes in front and five in hind prints. Front toes point slightly inward producing a "K" shaped print, while rear toes slope upward and outward.

Raccoon

FRONT

REAR

Five toes resembles hand of a baby. Front print smaller (1-3") with C-shaped heel pad. Rear print longer (1.5-4") heel pad.

Opossum

FRONT   REAR

Five fingers and human hand shape. Opposable thumbs on hind feet.

Rabbit

REAR

FRONT

Larger hind feet, smaller front feet. Hoppers producing a "Y" shaped track.

Skunk

FRONT   REAR

Five toes on their hind and front feet. Front and rear are approximately same size. Claws show up in many prints.

Otter

FRONT   REAR

Five toes and short claws give their prints a pointed look. Toes are partially webbed.

Armadillo

REAR

FRONT

Four long toe prints with sharp claw at tip. Front print show distinct "V" between middle toes.

Sketch

_____
_____
_____
_____
_____
_____
_____
_____
_____
_____
_____

General

Date: _____ Location: _____

Environment: ⬭ Mud ⬭ Snow ⬭ Soft Garden Soil ⬭ Sand

Time of Day: ⬭ Morning ⬭ Midday ⬭ Evening ⬭ Time_____

Front Toes: ⬭ Five ⬭ Four ⬭ Three ⬭ Two

Rear Toes: ⬭ Five ⬭ Four ⬭ Three ⬭ Two

Track Symmetry: ⬭ Symmetric ⬭ Asymmetric

Claws / Nails: ⬭ Visible ⬭ Not Visible   Webbing: ⬭ Yes ⬭ No

Surroundings: _____

Movement Pattern: ⬭ Zig-Zaggler ⬭ Trot ⬭ Lope ⬭ Gallop

Notes: _____

Canine

Wolf

FRONT   REAR

Biggest in this group with a long (4") and wide print.

Coyote
FRONT   REAR

Slightly smaller than wolves with print more narrow (2.5 to 3.5").

Fox
FRONT   REAR

Smallest in the group with print (2 to 3") and fuzzy around edges.

Dog
FRONT   REAR

Similar to wolf/coyote with thicker nails.

Feline

Cougar / Mountain Lion

FRONT   REAR

Largest in the group (greater than 3"). Size of domestic dog.

Lynx
FRONT   REAR

Same as cougar but smaller in size and not as defined due to fur around paws.

Bobcat

FRONT   REAR

Smaller tracks (2"). Often confused with coyote or fox but lacks nails. Round shape.

House Cat

FRONT   REAR

Small (1 to 1.5"). Similar to domestic dog, meander when walking.

Bird

Crow

Standard bird track: 3 forward, 1 rear. Print 2-2.5".

Grouse

Small ground birds with only 3 forward toes. Print 2" long.

Turkey

Similar to grouse but much larger prints (4") long.

Duck

Webbing gives its print distinctive shape.

Bear

Black Bear

FRONT   REAR

Has short claws and its toes spread out in a curve over its foot pad. Generally going to be smaller than grizzly bear paw.

Grizzly Bear

FRONT   REAR

Has long claws that extend out further from their toes. Its toes also are held closer together, forming almost a straight line above the foot pad.

Rodent

Beaver

FRONT   REAR
Webbed hind feet with 5 toes (4.5-7"). Sometime 4-toed prints.

Porcupine
FRONT REAR
Usually only see pads in prints (1-2"). Pigeon-toed.

Muskrat

FRONT   REAR
Hand-like like raccoon but smaller (2.3").

Mouse
FRONT   REAR
Larger back feet (1.5 - 2"), smaller front feet (0.25-0.5").

Squirrel

FRONT   REAR
Larger back feet (1.5-2"), smaller front feet (1-1.5").

Hoof

Mountain Goat

FRONT   REAR
Have toes that spread when they step, creating a distinctive V shape at the top of their print.

Bighorn Sheep

FRONT   REAR
Similar to deer but with straighter edges and less pointed. More blocky and less shaped like a heart.

Wild Hog

FRONT   REAR
Often confused with deer but toes are wider, rounder and blunter and don't come to a point. Have dew claw that rests slightly outside print.

Reptile / Amphibian

Alligator

FRONT
REAR
Large feet with four toes on front prints and five toes on rear prints. Front are wide in heel, rear are longer, narrow and pointed heel.

Lizard

FRONT   REAR
Lightweight and don't leave much of a track. Might leave small scuff from feet and small tail drag.

Frog

FRONT   REAR
Have four bulbous toes in front and five in hind prints. Front toes point slightly inward producing a "K" shaped print, while rear toes slope upward and outward.

Other Common

Raccoon

FRONT
REAR
Five toes resembles hand of a baby. Front print smaller (1-3") with C-shaped heel pad. Rear print longer (1.5-4") heel pad.

Opossum

FRONT   REAR
Five fingers and human hand shape. Opposable thumbs on hind feet.

Rabbit

REAR
FRONT
Larger hind feet, smaller front feet. Hoppers producing a "Y" shaped track.

Skunk

FRONT
REAR
Five toes on their hind and front feet. Front and rear are approximately same size. Claws show up in many prints.

Otter

FRONT   REAR
Five toes and short claws give their prints a pointed look. Toes are partially webbed.

Armadillo

REAR
FRONT
Four long toe prints with sharp claw at tip. Front print show distinct "V" between middle toes.

Sketch

Sketch / Notes

General

Date: _____ Location: _____

Environment: ◯ Mud   ◯ Snow   ◯ Soft Garden Soil   ◯ Sand

Time of Day: ◯ Morning   ◯ Midday   ◯ Evening   ◯ Time _____

Front Toes: ◯ Five   ◯ Four   ◯ Three   ◯ Two

Rear Toes: ◯ Five   ◯ Four   ◯ Three   ◯ Two

Track Symmetry: ◯ Symmetric   ◯ Asymmetric

Claws / Nails: ◯ Visible   ◯ Not Visible   Webbing: ◯ Yes   ◯ No

Surroundings: _____

Movement Pattern: ◯ Zig-Zaggler   ◯ Trot   ◯ Lope   ◯ Gallop

Notes: _____

Canine

Wolf

FRONT   REAR

Biggest in this group with a long (4") and wide print.

Coyote
FRONT   REAR

Slightly smaller than wolves with print more narrow (2.5 to 3.5").

Fox
FRONT   REAR

Smallest in the group with print (2 to 3") and fuzzy around edges.

Dog
FRONT   REAR

Similar to wolf/coyote with thicker nails.

Feline

Cougar / Mountain Lion
FRONT   REAR

Largest in the group (greater than 3"). Size of domestic dog.

Lynx
FRONT   REAR

Same as cougar but smaller in size and not as defined due to fur around paws.

Bobcat
FRONT   REAR

Smaller tracks (2"). Often confused with coyote or fox but lacks nails. Round shape.

House Cat
FRONT   REAR

Small (1 to 1.5"). Similar to domestic dog, meander when walking.

Bird

Crow
Standard bird track: 3 forward, 1 rear. Print 2-2.5".

Grouse
Small ground birds with only 3 forward toes. Print 2" long.

Turkey
Similar to grouse but much larger prints (4") long.

Duck
Webbing gives its print distinctive shape.

Bear

Black Bear
FRONT   REAR

Has short claws and its toes spread out in a curve over its foot pad. Generally going to be smaller than grizzly bear paw.

Grizzly Bear
FRONT   REAR

Has long claws that extend out further from their toes. Its toes also are held closer together, forming almost a straight line above the foot pad.

Rodent

Beaver

FRONT   REAR
Webbed hind feet with 5 toes (4.5-7"). Sometime 4-toed prints.

Porcupine

FRONT   REAR
Usually only see pads in prints (1-2"). Pigeon-toed.

Muskrat

FRONT   REAR
Hand-like like raccoon but smaller (2.3").

Mouse

FRONT   REAR
Larger back feet (1.5 - 2"), smaller front feet (0.25-0.5").

Squirrel

FRONT   REAR
Larger back feet (1.5-2"), smaller front feet (1-1.5').

Hoof

Mountain Goat

FRONT   REAR
Have toes that spread when they step, creating a distinctive V shape at the top of their print.

Bighorn Sheep

FRONT   REAR
Similar to deer but with straighter edges and less pointed. More blocky and less shaped like a heart.

Wild Hog

FRONT   REAR
Often confused with deer but toes are wider, rounder and blunter and don't come to a point. Have dew claw that rests slightly outside print.

Reptile / Amphibian

Alligator

FRONT
REAR
Large feet with four toes on front prints and five toes on rear prints. Front are wide in heel, rear are longer, narrow and pointed heel.

Lizard

FRONT   REAR
Lightweight and don't leave much of a track. Might leave small scuff from feet and small tail drag.

Frog

FRONT   REAR
Have four bulbous toes in front and five in hind prints. Front toes point slightly inward producing a "K" shaped print, while rear toes slope upward and outward.

Other Common

Raccoon

FRONT
REAR
Five toes resembles hand of a baby. Front print smaller (1-3") with C-shaped heel pad. Rear print longer (1.5-4") heel pad.

Opossum

FRONT   REAR
Five fingers and human hand shape. Opposable thumbs on hind feet.

Rabbit
REAR

FRONT
Larger hind feet, smaller front feet. Hoppers producing a "Y" shaped track.

Skunk

FRONT
REAR
Five toes on their hind and front feet. Front and rear are approximately same size. Claws show up in many prints.

Otter

FRONT   REAR
Five toes and short claws give their prints a pointed look. Toes are partially webbed.

Armadillo
REAR
FRONT
Four long toe prints with sharp claw at tip. Front print show distinct "V" between middle toes.

Sketch / Notes

Sketch

_____
_____
_____
_____
_____
_____
_____
_____
_____
_____
_____

General

Date: _____ Location: _____

Environment: ◯ Mud ◯ Snow ◯ Soft Garden Soil ◯ Sand

Time of Day: ◯ Morning ◯ Midday ◯ Evening ◯ Time_____

Front Toes: ◯ Five ◯ Four ◯ Three ◯ Two

Rear Toes: ◯ Five ◯ Four ◯ Three ◯ Two

Track Symmetry: ◯ Symmetric ◯ Asymmetric

Claws / Nails: ◯ Visible ◯ Not Visible Webbing: ◯ Yes ◯ No

Surroundings: _____

Movement Pattern: ◯ Zig-Zaggler ◯ Trot ◯ Lope ◯ Gallop

Notes: _____

Canine

Wolf
FRONT REAR
Biggest in this group with a long (4") and wide print.

Coyote
FRONT REAR
Slightly smaller than wolves with print more narrow (2.5 to 3.5").

Fox
FRONT REAR
Smallest in the group with print (2 to 3") and fuzzy around edges.

Dog
FRONT REAR
Similar to wolf/coyote with thicker nails.

Feline

Cougar / Mountain Lion
FRONT REAR
Largest in the group (greater than 3"). Size of domestic dog.

Lynx
FRONT REAR
Same as cougar but smaller in size and not as defined due to fur around paws.

Bobcat
FRONT REAR
Smaller tracks (2"). Often confused with coyote or fox but lacks nails. Round shape.

House Cat
FRONT REAR
Small (1 to 1.5"). Similar to domestic dog, meander when walking.

Bird

Crow
Standard bird track: 3 forward, 1 rear. Print 2-2.5".

Grouse
Small ground birds with only 3 forward toes. Print 2" long.

Turkey
Similar to grouse but much larger prints (4") long.

Duck
Webbing gives its print distinctive shape.

Bear

Black Bear
FRONT REAR
Has short claws and its toes spread out in a curve over its foot pad. Generally going to be smaller than grizzly bear paw.

Grizzly Bear
FRONT REAR
Has long claws that extend out further from their toes. Its toes also are held closer together, forming almost a straight line above the foot pad.

Rodent

Beaver

FRONT REAR

Webbed hind feet with 5 toes (4.5-7"). Sometime 4-toed prints.

Porcupine
FRONT REAR

Usually only see pads in prints (1-2"). Pigeon-toed.

Muskrat

FRONT REAR

Hand-like like raccoon but smaller (2.3").

Mouse

FRONT REAR

Larger back feet (1.5 - 2"), smaller front feet (0.25-0.5").

Squirrel

FRONT REAR

Larger back feet (1.5-2"), smaller front feet (1-1.5").

Hoof

Mountain Goat

FRONT REAR

Have toes that spread when they step, creating a distinctive V shape at the top of their print.

Bighorn Sheep

FRONT REAR

Similar to deer but with straighter edges and less pointed. More blocky and less shaped like a heart.

Wild Hog

FRONT REAR

Often confused with deer but toes are wider, rounder and blunter and don't come to a point. Have dew claw that rests slightly outside print.

Reptile / Amphibian

Alligator

FRONT
REAR

Large feet with four toes on front prints and five toes on rear prints. Front are wide in heel, rear are longer, narrow and pointed heel.

Lizard

FRONT REAR

Lightweight and don't leave much of a track. Might leave small scuff from feet and small tail drag.

Frog

FRONT REAR

Have four bulbous toes in front and five in hind prints. Front toes point slightly inward producing a "K" shaped print, while rear toes slope upward and outward.

Other Common

Raccoon

FRONT
REAR

Five toes resembles hand of a baby. Front print smaller (1-3") with C-shaped heel pad. Rear print longer (1.5-4") heel pad.

Opossum

FRONT REAR

Five fingers and human hand shape. Opposable thumbs on hind feet .

Rabbit
REAR

FRONT

Larger hind feet, smaller front feet. Hoppers producing a "Y" shaped track.

Skunk

FRONT
REAR

Five toes on their hind and front feet. Front and rear are approximately same size. Claws show up in many prints.

Otter

FRONT REAR

Five toes and short claws give their prints a pointed look. Toes are partially webbed.

Armadillo
REAR
FRONT

Four long toe prints with sharp claw at tip. Front print show distinct "V" between middle toes.

Sketch

Sketch / Notes

_____
_____
_____
_____
_____
_____
_____
_____
_____
_____
_____
_____

General

Date: _____   Location: _____

Environment: ◯ Mud   ◯ Snow   ◯ Soft Garden Soil   ◯ Sand

Time of Day: ◯ Morning   ◯ Midday   ◯ Evening   ◯ Time _____

Front Toes: ◯ Five   ◯ Four   ◯ Three   ◯ Two

Rear Toes: ◯ Five   ◯ Four   ◯ Three   ◯ Two

Track Symmetry: ◯ Symmetric   ◯ Asymmetric

Claws / Nails: ◯ Visible   ◯ Not Visible   Webbing: ◯ Yes   ◯ No

Surroundings: _____

Movement Pattern: ◯ Zig-Zaggler   ◯ Trot   ◯ Lope   ◯ Gallop

Notes: _____

Canine

Wolf

FRONT   REAR

Biggest in this group with a long (4") and wide print.

Coyote

FRONT   REAR

Slightly smaller than wolves with print more narrow (2.5 to 3.5").

Fox

FRONT   REAR

Smallest in the group with print (2 to 3") and fuzzy around edges.

Dog

FRONT   REAR

Similar to wolf/coyote with thicker nails.

Feline

Cougar / Mountain Lion

FRONT   REAR

Largest in the group (greater than 3"). Size of domestic dog.

Lynx

FRONT   REAR

Same as cougar but smaller in size and not as defined due to fur around paws.

Bobcat

FRONT   REAR

Smaller tracks (2"). Often confused with coyote or fox but lacks nails. Round shape.

House Cat

FRONT   REAR

Small (1 to 1.5"). Similar to domestic dog, meander when walking.

Bird

Crow

Standard bird track: 3 forward, 1 rear. Print 2-2.5".

Grouse

Small ground birds with only 3 forward toes. Print 2" long.

Turkey

Similar to grouse but much larger prints (4") long.

Duck

Webbing gives its print distinctive shape.

Bear

Black Bear

FRONT   REAR

Has short claws and its toes spread out in a curve over its foot pad. Generally going to be smaller than grizzly bear paw.

Grizzly Bear

FRONT   REAR

Has long claws that extend out further from their toes. Its toes also are held closer together, forming almost a straight line above the foot pad.

Rodent

Beaver

FRONT · REAR
Webbed hind feet with 5 toes (4.5-7"). Sometime 4-toed prints.

Porcupine

FRONT · REAR
Usually only see pads in prints (1-2"). Pigeon-toed.

Muskrat

FRONT · REAR
Hand-like like raccoon but smaller (2.3").

Mouse

FRONT · REAR
Larger back feet (1.5 - 2"), smaller front feet (0.25-0.5").

Squirrel
FRONT · REAR
Larger back feet (1.5-2"), smaller front feet (1-1.5").

Hoof

Mountain Goat

FRONT · REAR
Have toes that spread when they step, creating a distinctive V shape at the top of their print.

Bighorn Sheep

FRONT · REAR
Similar to deer but with straighter edges and less pointed. More blocky and less shaped like a heart.

Wild Hog

FRONT · REAR
Often confused with deer but toes are wider, rounder and blunter and don't come to a point. Have dew claw that rests slightly outside print.

Reptile / Amphibian

Alligator

FRONT · REAR
Large feet with four toes on front prints and five toes on rear prints. Front are wide in heel, rear are longer, narrow and pointed heel.

Lizard

FRONT · REAR
Lightweight and don't leave much of a track. Might leave small scuff from feet and small tail drag.

Frog

FRONT · REAR
Have four bulbous toes in front and five in hind prints. Front toes point slightly inward producing a "K" shaped print, while rear toes slope upward and outward.

Other Common

Raccoon

FRONT · REAR
Five toes resembles hand of a baby. Front print smaller (1-3") with C-shaped heel pad. Rear print longer (1.5-4") heel pad.

Opossum

FRONT · REAR
Five fingers and human hand shape. Opposable thumbs on hind feet.

Rabbit
 REAR · FRONT
Larger hind feet, smaller front feet. Hoppers producing a "Y" shaped track.

Skunk

FRONT · REAR
Five toes on their hind and front feet. Front and rear are approximately same size. Claws show up in many prints.

Otter

FRONT · REAR
Five toes and short claws give their prints a pointed look. Toes are partially webbed.

Armadillo
 REAR · FRONT
Four long toe prints with sharp claw at tip. Front print show distinct "V" between middle toes.

Sketch

Sketch / Notes

_____
_____
_____
_____
_____
_____
_____
_____
_____
_____
_____

Made in the USA
Las Vegas, NV
19 February 2024

85980216R00066